BUILDING CHAMPIONSHIP CROSS COUNTRY PROGRAMS

Doug Soles

ISBN-13: 9798372119963
ISBN-10: 1477123456

Cover design by: Doug Soles
Library of Congress Control Number: 2018675309
Printed in the United States of America

To the many athletes that chose to dedicate their time, energy, and focus in the success of the Great Oak Cross Country program over the years. Your hard work and passion have fueled me as a coach each season! Whether you were our fastest superstar, or our most basic beginner, you have helped build a program that embodies hard work and dedication to the sport. I couldn't be prouder of the Great Oak distance runner and dedicate this book to their passion for constant improvement and love of the sport.

FOREWORD

I had the good fortune to hear Coach Doug Soles speak at an LA84 Clinic here in Southern California sometime back around 2007 or so. As you'll learn in the following pages, Doug is confident, knowledgeable, and not only determined to win, but to also help other coaches up their game. Nothing makes Doug Soles happier than competition, so sharing the methodologies that have worked to make his teams the best in America is a natural adjunct to his coaching. I had no idea who in the world Doug Soles was before I first heard him lead that clinic these many years ago, but I came away so impressed with his presentation that I used the lecture handouts to transform my own nascent cross country program. That meant more mileage, more commitment on the part of myself and my runners, and the emphatic belief that any team that puts in the work can rise to the top. Several California state championships later, I can honestly say that I would not be as audacious in my approach to training and coaching were it not for Doug Soles.

I warn you that not everyone is going to love this book. If you are a mediocre coach who clicks the stopwatch just for the paycheck, Doug's message of making your team a dominant force by a zealous refusal to lose may be extremely offensive. There's a very good chance you will hurl *Building Championship Cross Country Programs* against a wall. But if you love cross country just as much as you love the athletes you coach, and you rightfully believe that courses like Mt. SAC and Van Cortland Park are cathedrals in their own right, and if the daily act of preparing workouts is your happy place, then this book may transform not just your program but you as an individual and a coach. *Building Championship Cross Country Programs* is a manifesto, daring you to be the very best you can be, rising above mediocrity to coach with a passion and dogged determination you may have never have experienced.

There are no halfway efforts to Doug Soles. He's an all-in kind of guy. Give him the chance and he will talk your ear off about coaching. Our sport needs this sort of optimism and focus, which is why I'm so glad Doug put his insights into this book for those unable to interact with him on a personal level. As one who writes for a living, as well as coaching high school cross country for almost twenty years, I enjoyed the structure and narrative arc of *Building Championship Cross Country Programs.* As these pages show, Coach Soles put as much effort into writing this book as he does crafting championship teams – and it shows. See you on the podium.

Martin Dugard

Rancho Santa Margarita, California

October 2020

CONTENTS

Title Page

Copyright

Dedication

Foreword

PART I: Becoming an Elite Cross Country Coach   1

Chapter One: Run THE Show!   4

Chapter Two: Focus, Dedication, and Drive   26

Chapter Three: Ignoring the Minutia in a Sea of Importance   39

Chapter Four: Adversity and Losing: What We Learn and How We Adapt   51

PART II: Building an Elite Team   70

Chapter Five: Outworking Your Peers   72

Chapter Six: Where Are We Going?   88

Chapter Seven: Training for Success   104

Chapter Eight: Networking and Relationships – The Power of Communication   130

PART III: Perfecting and Maintaining an Elite Culture   138

Chapter Nine: World Domination – Why Winning Matters   141

Chapter Ten: Offering a Better Product – How to Convince Athletes to Follow You   154

Chapter Eleven: Consistency: How Great Oak Won 14 Out   167 of 20 State Championships in a Decade

Chapter Twelve: Final Thoughts 185

Conclusion 205

Afterword 207

Epilogue 209

Acknowledgement 223

About The Author 225

PART I: BECOMING AN ELITE CROSS COUNTRY COACH

This book was written in 2020, during the pandemic when I was still the head coach at Great Oak High School. As you read it, look at it through my eyes as the coach of that school during that time.

This isn't a training book - there are plenty of those out there. This book is about becoming the best coach you can become. It is about building a team that is always in contention to win, year after year. As you read, understand that it is designed as a challenge to you to become the best coach you can possibly become so that you can build the best programs you can possibly create. It is set up for you to challenge every belief you have ever had about being a coach. Somethings will make you better, some things you will already do. Take away from it that you can be better. Let me show you how!

When I got into coaching it was as an extension of my competitive juices that had flowed tremendously as a youth. Nobody tells you when you get older that the games are going to be replaced with work. Nobody tells you the days of nonstop competing are going to take a backseat to making a living. I wasn't ready for that. I wanted to find something in my life to fill that void, whether it was playing poker or looking for another outlet. I chanced into it with cross country. The journey it has taken me on has shown me that the competitive nature a person has can really pay off if you are willing to dedicate yourself to going all in as a coach.

Napoleon famously said, "If you want to take the island, burn the boats." To be a great coach you have to commit at that level. If you are a teacher first, father first, husband first, parishioner in your church first, then when are you a coach? At some point you have to decide what you are trying to build, and sacrifices will need to be made. Very rarely will you see someone who is elite in their sport or field, and they just got lucky. They just rolled in and happened to be able to high jump 7' 6," or just knew how to do open heart surgery. It doesn't work that way 99% of the time. How it works is that you go all in; you give everything you've got to building something special. When you do that, you will end up season after season getting a little bit better. If you stick with that passion long enough, you will build a championship team. Nothing is going to be given to you, and you should expect nothing to be given. It should be a grueling process, full of ups and downs, injuries and illnesses, wins and losses. Because that journey is truly where you find your true victory. Burn the ships, and commit to being the best coach you can be.

I've always felt like average doesn't apply to me. That isn't to say I'm not average at things; it means that I don't think in an average way. I will not lower myself to the average in the areas I'm trying to excel at. If I am going to be a pizza delivery guy, I'm going to be the guy that knows all the fastest routes to locations, delivers the most pizzas, and makes the most money. That is just how I'm wired. Average doesn't apply to me. I don't allow it. Many people shoot for the average. You know why? Average is comfortable. You don't stand out; nobody is watching you or judging you. You can blend in and do your thing comfortably. The problem is that comfort doesn't win anything! If you are comfortable with where you are, then your team isn't improving. You need to be uncomfortable, and looking for solutions in most areas of coaching. Why? Because this is an ever-evolving sport, with tons of new data coming out all the time. Immerse yourself in greatness, and do everything you can to avoid falling into the trap of being an average coach.

As you read through this book, challenge yourself to take an honest look at your program and the efforts that are put in. Could you give more? What sacrifices do you need to make to get to the next level? Are you building a fun team or a championship team? This book has been written as a guide for coaches who want to fill in the gaps in team building. To take a look at a program objectively and say "what am I missing that could take my group to the next level?" If you want to be an elite coach, with an elite team, then read through every page of this book with a highlighter out. Be prepared to challenge what your norm is, and be willing to take risks. Being elite is about not only being uncomfortable, but about making people around you uncomfortable as well. Winning comes from doing the things that nobody else around you are willing to do. Take charge, run the show, and become the coach you envision in your head. That is the first step to building a championship program!

CHAPTER ONE:
RUN THE SHOW!

Run the Show! Now this sounds like a top down, do as I say mantra that coaches from the 1950's used and drummed into their athletes like generals on the battlefield. The truth is that it isn't about that at all. It is about making sure, at all times, everyone around you knows and trusts who is in charge. When you are wholly in charge, nobody questions it. When every single person on your campus knows that you run the show, you make the decisions, you are where the buck stops, then a lot of the little issues that can arise will start to go away. I'm never looking for a fight, but I never hesitate to make sure the people around me know who is going to make the decision.

To build an elite program, you need to recruit talented athletes, hire good assistants, set forth a road map to where you want to be, and put in the time to get everyone there. You are the head coach. You are the KEY to the whole operation! The decisions that you make will determine the outcomes that happen around you. That means that you will make the easy decisions, but you will make all the hard ones too. At the end of the day, everyone you come in contact with has to know that you are in charge, that you run the show!

"Leave no doubt." I often tell this to my assistant coaches. Leave no doubt who is in charge. Not by being mean, or yelling a lot, or telling people you are in charge. The key to running the show is being the most prepared person at all times. You know what is going on, you hold the keys to the training schedule and the workouts that will happen that day, and you are two steps ahead of everyone else. When you can tell an athlete, what is going to happen, and then it happens, they will realize that you are the one that is the most bought in, the one who cares the most. Nobody questions the person with all the knowledge, all the passion, all the focus, and all the preparation. People question you when you are unprepared. Take being the head coach seriously, and make sure that everyone around you realizes that you are in charge, because you are the person who should be in charge. You are the one who should be the captain of this ship. Eliminate doubt, and eliminate it early on. This is your show and everyone knows it.

Insights to Become a Better Coach

I want you to think about where you are currently as a coach. Is it where you want to be? Do you want to take your coaching to the next level? Do you want to start competing against better teams? Throughout this book I will help you identify key areas where you are lacking, or things that you need to implement or improve to make those moves up to the next level as a coach. As you read, try to find components that you are missing in your program, or that are underdeveloped so that you can improve those areas. Coaches that build programs that have very few areas that need improvement will consistently be producing some of the best talent in their area and beyond. This doesn't happen overnight, but with enough time, effort, and focus it will happen for you.

Every head cross country coach in the country is effectively the Chief Executive Officer of a mini corporation. We have costs and we bring in revenue, we have workers, we have a mission statement, and we are trying to be the best. As the CEO, you will determine which direction the program will take, who to hire, who to fire, and ultimately which of your workers will best represent your program in competitions. You define the success, and every single program will define success differently. This isn't a small little get together of runners, this is a full time business and you have to run it like one.

What is the difference between building a team versus building a program? A team is part of a program, the girls team or the boys team combined make up a program. If you are a coach that has both halves, you are building a program. If you have one gender or the other, you are building a team. This is a small identification difference, but an important one to note. A girls team can change in a heartbeat, with just a couple good frosh girls completely rewriting your top 7 instantly. Boys' teams tend to change over time, as you develop a good class to be competitive when they are older. Building a team is different, because you are not beholden to the other half and the differences between coaching each gender. If you only coach boys, you can ignore a lot of the things that go into successfully coaching a girls team. This is the same if you only coach girls, and don't have to worry about the boys team. To build a successful program, you have to establish the tenets in your philosophy and how you address your group that covers both teams, and does it without alienating one for the other. You have to deal with being equal. If one team gets something, so does the other one. You have to share your time with both, and they have to know that you care as much for one side as you do for the other. Elite coaches are masters at getting any athlete they are working with to find success, regardless of gender or age. As you build your team or program, be thinking about what things you can do to ensure that the group you are working with is special. They aren't second class to the other team, they aren't ignored because they aren't good that year, and they don't have to be better than some team from the past. Be a team that has its own identity and build it to thrive.

Want it more than other coaches do. Seems obvious, right? The truth that I have come to discover is that not every coach you are competing against wants it that bad. Many just want to be a part of something. Your job is to want success for your program more than anyone else does. To set a bar at a level only a maniac could achieve, and then formulate a plan to reach it. Wanting it more means that you will put in the time, the effort, and the overall learning it takes to move up the coaching scale. If you are constantly getting the same results and doing the same things, something has to change. Keep doing what you always do and you will always get similar results. What happens if you up your mileage from 35 miles a week on average to 50? What happens if you go from zero doubles a week, to three days of doubles during a training week? What happens if you spend 10 hours more over the summer emailing and calling incoming 9th graders. What about 50 more hours? Wanting it more means everything takes a back seat to finding the next athlete to change your results. You are the only person who can do that. Want it more than your peers do.

Comfortability in what we do can be the most obstructive part of our improving as a coach. Challenge yourself to try new things, reflect, adjust, try again. Not with one item, but with lots of them. One of the biggest problem's coaches have is they get satisfied. They win a couple league or district titles and now believe their training plan is a success. It has been successful, so therefore it is a good training plan. The problem with that is your athletes might be succeeding in spite of your training, rather than because of it. You get a couple good classes back to back and anyone can win for a few years, especially at a local level. Some leagues just aren't very good, so coaching at a mediocre level will allow you to succeed. Any average coach can look like a superstar coach when they have a highly talented athlete. Success is what you choose it to be, but if you want to move to the elite level, there is no amount of success that will ever satisfy you. You will always be frustrated that this frosh didn't sign up, or this race was slower than we thought it would be. This always forces you to reevaluate what you are doing and allows you to reimagine changes to your program. Don't be satisfied, but instead look to improve in every facet of your program, always. Don't be comfortable. Comfortability breeds average, and average doesn't win anything.

Honor your promises. If I tell an athlete that they will be running in the top 7 at a specific meet, and then change it when we get to that point, I have broken my word to that athlete, and in the long run that athlete won't trust me. Many times, I have made decisions that weren't the best because I had to honor my word. What I have learned from this is that athletes will trust you when you are honest and they won't when you go back on your word, even if it is justifiable in your eyes to make changes for the betterment of the team. Sometimes you just have to take the loss and make the adjustment at a later date. Do not make promises that you don't plan to keep, and make sure to keep the promises that you make to athletes!

There is a fundamental need by cross country athletes to have a belief in their coaching staff, their training program, and the work that they are being asked to do. Your job as a head coach is to not only put those items in place, but to ensure everyone running for you that you are the one that will get them where they want to go. Elite coaches are often pied pipers. They are people that you can't help but follow because they see the vision in their head so clearly and can share that vision with those around them. Many coaches want to be secret about everything they do, believing that doing that keeps the power with them. The truth is, to be an elite coach you need to empower everyone around you. Empower your athletes to learn the sport, to learn to make decisions and give feedback and input on the big decisions they may have to make later in their careers. Empower your assistant coaches to lead their groups. You guide them, but you also listen to them. Listen to their feedback and feed off their energy. Some of the best coaches in the US are assistant coaches! Not everybody has the time, energy, or personal strength to lead, but many find a way to contribute and assist others on the journey. Find and utilize people's talents to make your program better. Empower your administration to trust you. Show them you can set the schedule, and not only can you set it, you can build a schedule that makes sense for your teams current and long-term development. Show your admin that you can lead your program with limited issues, and when issues arise, you can handle those situations. Empower people to believe in you, because when they do you will be able to accomplish more than you ever realized you could!

Expectations

There are four main expectations that I have for my athletes at each practice:

- Show up every day.

- Do what we ask you to do.

- Do it with a smile on your face.

- Be a good teammate.

These simple concepts have built the foundation of the best cross country teams in California and US history. Many coaches overthink what they need to convey to their athletes, but the truth is what you really want to do is teach your athletes what they need to do and get out of their way. Elite coaches aren't drill sergeants, and they aren't screamers. Elite coaches are people that have figured out that each season they get a different group to take on a journey, and that their goal is to guide those athletes to the place they are hoping to get to. The key to that is keeping it simple. Be here. Be consistent in the things we are asking of you. Keep a positive attitude towards what we are doing. Any coach that can instill those three expectations in their athletes is able to take a step back and watch, listen, and position the direction of the team instead of trying to force the group to go a direction they may not yet be willing to go to.

One of the best ways to tell if you are pushing your team, or if you are guiding them is to take a step back and watch practice with limited interaction from you. No instruction, just let the athletes do what they are supposed to do. Does bedlam ensue? Does their effort go down? If so, they may be relying on you to provide what they need to provide for themselves. They need to wake up in the morning seeing the success they want to have, not the work they have to do for a taskmaster. By becoming a guide, you are telling your team that you trust them to do what they believe is the right thing. You are telling them that you trust their instincts, you trust their vision and goals as much as you trust your own. There is nothing more powerful than watching a group of athletes control a practice from start to finish without realizing that you aren't giving them instruction. They know what to do and are there because they want to accomplish it.

When you are a guide, you are there to nudge the athletes the right direction when they start to go the wrong direction, and they will go the wrong direction from time to time. Subtle correction, built on trust and partnership allows for you to push things a little more this way or a little more that way when needed. The athletes may not even notice you doing it, and that is a good thing. The more ownership of their goals they have, the more engaged they will stay on the journey. Dennis Rodman worked with the Chicago Bulls because Phil Jackson didn't freak out every time Dennis took off. Instead, he nudged Dennis back into position, kept everyone around him calm, and kept the focus on the team goals. Your job as guide isn't to force things, it is to know when to speak, and when to listen. It is to pull a kid aside in private and put them back on the right path if they start to veer. Winning comes with elite athletes, and elite athletes by nature means ego management. Keep your team focused on the perceived issues outside the team, so that you don't end up with issues on your team.

As a coach there will be moments of intensity, heat of the moment battles, horrible decisions made by others around you. Your job is to know when to bend everyone to your will and when to sit back and let things happen. Sometimes you can't sit back and nudge things into place. Sometimes everyone needs a wakeup call that things are traveling in a direction that is counter to the stated goals of the team. That is when you shift gears. You see this often in poker tournaments, where players will sit back hand after hand waiting for the right cards or the right moment to make a move or change the pace of how they are playing. When everyone starts playing tight trying to make it to the next round of the tournament, that is when you attack and start picking up pots because nobody else wants to engage and risk not moving on. As a coach, you have to know when to shift gears and change from a guide that is everyone's best friend to a motivator that could sell fire to the devil. In small moments, those will be the parts of the journey that everyone remembers, because you do it when it matters and you do it out of love.

Taking Inventory of What You Have and What You Are Missing

Every single high school in America is unique. There are so many factors that go into consistent success at the elite level, that you must take an inventory of what you have going for you and what you must bend to your will. The United States education system is not designed in many areas to fully support athletics like a European club system does. Often, we as educators have to make things happen in our own schools to get our team to the next level. If you are waiting for someone else at your school to make it happen for you, it won't ever happen. You have to be the one pushing for the things you need. What are the factors of your situation that you are missing that could make the difference in the success of your program? Let's explore some of the key factors below.

At the elite level there are a lot of little things that can separate you from your closest competitors. EliptiGO bikes, massage guns, gear sponsorships, or the ability to make your own schedule with lots of travel in it can be the difference between you having a competitive team, or an elite team. Ask yourself, what am I missing that would help us improve? What can I better utilize to advance our team or program?

- **School Population** – This is probably the biggest factor in long term success as a cross country coach. Even an average coach can consistently be pretty good at a large school with lots of talent each season. With that being said, I can name a lot of schools that I compete with that have a school that should be successful, but it isn't. Population can give you an advantage, but it is what you do with that advantage that makes the biggest difference. Use this advantage and build the biggest program you can! If you have a small school, you will have to maximize the population that you get, which means sharing athletes with other sports and being flexible with club athlete's schedules. No matter what, find a way to get kids running races for you.

- **Enough Practice Time** – How much practice time do you need to fit in all of the components your team needs to be successful each day. We spend

30 minutes in the morning and 2:30 in the afternoon. I would still take more time if they would give it to me. How much are you allowed? Can you get a 1st Period XC/Track PE class that will give you more time to build mileage and add doubles to your program (instead of an end of the day sports class)? What can athletes do on their own at home to get better? Practice time matters, utilize every bit of time you have. Outside of working out, you still need to have meetings, watch videos, do visualizations, etc. Don't give away time to get better, maximize it!!!

- **Administrative Support** – I have been blessed to have had a lot of supportive administrators in my time as a coach. That doesn't mean all are, and administrators in some areas change every 2-3 years. Building support with administration means that you show them that you are a leader and that your program has few issues. It means that you can manage the budget and set the schedule and they know it. It means that you can go in and discuss the issues that arise, but still be an advocate for your team. Don't go in and argue a problem, go in with a list of solutions to a problem and make decision making easy for admin. They don't want to deal with your issues, make it easy on them and you will find that you have fewer and fewer issues as the years go by. If you do get an administrator that you don't click with and your admin cycles through quickly, then wait them out. Head coaches go through a lot of principals through the years, they will probably be gone before you will. Do your best to give your admin reasons to not only support you and your team, but to cheer for your success!

- **Enough Assistant Coaches** – Assistant coaches are all around you. Teachers, parents, alums, and that guy that is always out running around town. There are any number of people that are willing to donate time to the cause if you would just ask them. Contrary to common belief, coaches don't need to know anything about running or coaching to start. They just have to want to be a part of your program and you have to find people that are all about kids! I've had multiple coaches that were just teachers on campus that the kids at the school liked, so I hired them. Most of them were instantly good coaches, because they knew how to teach, and they knew how to interact with children. Ironically, many will coach for free or for the team gear. I try to have anywhere from 5-7 assistant coaches for cross country a year for a team of 150+ athletes. It allows me to set up groups (I still do the workouts for all groups), and for the assistants to have a group to develop for me. Nobody wants to stand there and watch you coach, find ways to empower them to impact the results on your team. Coaches want to watch an athlete finish a race and know they played a role in that success. If money is an issue, fundraise more or find a sponsor! That is an excuse, if you need more coaches, you will find the money!

- **Parental Support** – Parents can make or break a team. It is your job to ensure the parents understand your role, and that they understand theirs. Make sure that you let them know what your plan is for the team, for their athlete, and what they can do to help you make those plans work. Working hand in hand with your parents can give you a big advantage financially, and also with your administration should any issues arise. Your job is to sell the vision so that they are there to support you when you need it! Give parents the opportunity to have some hand in the success of the program.

- **Program Finances** – Not every team is going to have a sponsorship or be able to collect fees or donations. If that is the case you will need to get creative in your fundraising. Do an email fundraiser where everyone on your team inputs 20 emails and your team sends out a "support us" email. These are quick and easy and usually bring in pretty large amounts. There are many companies like Snap! and Reaching Our Goal that do most of the work for you. Other great options like car washes, breakfast tickets, drawings for vacations or iPads, jog-a-thons, or meal nights at local restaurants all can bring in some serious money for your team. To be elite you should be traveling, and that costs money, sometimes big money. Put your amazing parent group or assistant coaches in charge of some of the fundraisers, but always support them if you want them to work. Build a big pot of money so that you always can do the things that this year's team wants to do without worry.

- **Better Talent** – Your team is only as good at the talent you have on it, right? If that is true, then you must do everything you can to get out the best talent your school has to offer. Every single summer you have a chance to fight for the athletes coming into your school. The more elite athletes you get out for your program, the better your chance has to compete with the best. Who is it that you are missing from your team right now that is walking your halls? What can you do to get them to join you? One athlete might be the difference between winning the state meet, or taking 10th. Try 400 runners from track, soccer or basketball kids that aren't getting playing time, and even athletes that you failed to get in years prior. Sometimes they get cut a year or two into the sport they originally were in and are looking for a new opportunity. I've had seasons where girls with 4:55 1600m PR's didn't make our top 7. You can never have too much talent!

- **Extra Equipment** – What extra equipment can you purchase that will help you develop athletes better? EliptiGO's/Stationary Bikes? Plyo Boxes? Med Balls? Garmin watches? Resistance bands? Make a list of the items you need to purchase to ensure you can develop athletes at the highest level possible. Give this list to your parents and empower them to get you the items you need.

- **Scheduling Ability** – Make sure that you are the one setting the schedule each season. A basic athletic director schedule will pair you up in dual and tri meets against random high schools that work for the AD, but not for you. If someone wants to schedule a basketball game with your school, the AD may say that they will take it on their schedule if the other AD takes a cross country and tennis schedule addition in return. This type of scheduling is NOT conducive to the success of your team! Make sure you and only you are in charge of setting the schedule for your program so that you can control the rhythm of your season. Schedule X number of league/dual/tri meets and X number of invitationals. X should equal the amount that makes sense for your program and allows you to control when you want your athletes to go hard, and when you want to hit a 2-3 week training block uninterrupted. If you are shooting to move to the elite level, then you have to travel and you have to take on the best teams in your region and beyond.

Take an inventory of your advantages and disadvantages. Put a group of people (parents, assistants, athletes, etc.) in charge of getting you what you need. If you need bikes for the injury group, get your parents to raise you the money for the bikes. If you need more athletes out, put together a crew of athletes in charge of walking the halls the first 2 weeks of school and signing up more athletes. Find your weaknesses and work hard to eliminate as many of them as you can each season. Identify your advantages, and look to exploit them to the fullest versus all the other teams you compete against. You should be on a yearly crusade to fix as many issues in your program as you can, while taking inventory of where you are at is critical in outlining what needs to be fixed.

Coaching is a Rhythm

One of the things I learned early on was that coaching and individual seasons have a rhythm to them. Hone your rhythm from season to season. Find out what happens when you do this or that and dial in the pieces that work. Make subtle changes. Some people call it trial and error, but I believe it is more than that. I believe that you can develop a rhythm to your seasons, that you can keep key meets, key workouts, and an understanding of when to push and when to rest your athletes so that they are ready at just the right times, and that you will know what to expect so that you can make adjustments as needed. Don't let others dictate to you what your rhythm is, work with your coaches and your athletes and find the rhythm for your program, as every team is different. Like a heartbeat or a song, each season has its own rhythm, its own ups and downs to it, and you are the one that guides it. Head coaches specifically control the direction that rhythm heads. Learn what works each season, dial in the components that you need to keep, get rid of the components that don't fit or didn't work. If you are going to consistently win in cross country, it can't be random. *It needs to be your symphony, and you need to be conducting.*

Every season has a coach's rhythm to it. When you feel good, when you don't, when you get sick, when your own family gets sick. Recognize and document the things you need to be prepared for that might take you out of the equation at practice or at meets. Are there meetings for your teaching subject that happen each year at a certain time? Vacations? What do you need to plan for or around to make sure you are ready? If you find that you are always extra tired at the start of October, then plan for that. Up your food intake, shorten your personal workouts, and have yourself in bed earlier during the build up to that time. The more prepared you are for your own personal rhythm, the better you can have yourself ready to coach at your maximum when it matters.

Determining your athlete's rhythm can be a little more complicated. When do you find them tired or fried? When are they crushing it? Why? As you find the answers to these questions, you can make adjustments for them that allow the rhythm to be smoother the following season. One year we decided we were only going to do a 3 week summer break and then hit it hard the rest of the season. This was very different than our usual starting point, which was about 6 weeks out from the end of school. The first thing I noticed was that by the time we got to October, our coaches and athletes were both done. Tired and ready for the season to end is the best way to describe it, but we still had almost two full months of the season remaining. The second issue was that we peaked much earlier than the year prior and had to try to hold on for a lot longer than the years before. Needless to say, that season did not end well. Every adjustment you make as a coach will have a positive or negative consequence to your seasonal rhythm for your athletes. Understand that some adjustments will throw off previously successful parts of your rhythm. As you find what works, makes small moves to try to get your athletes mentally and physically ready for the most important meets.

The seasonal rhythm of the team has to do with how it is scheduled, when you will allow your athletes to go all out, versus when you are keeping them controlled, or when you want them to feel the best. We often refer to peaking as athletes running at their best, but often it is just that we get them to the line at their maximum level of freshness, while they are fit. Allowing them to be fresh when we want them to run well gives the coaching staff a little more control over how the athlete sees the end of the season, and how the overall peak looks to everyone watching. To control your seasonal rhythm, focus on setting a schedule that gives you control of when and where you will be going all out, when you will need to use your A team versus using the B team, and when you can rest and train through to get the desired effect at the end of the season. Typically, your top athletes should only be asked to go all-out effort wise 3-5 times before the state meet. Many coaches make the mistake of having their top athletes go hard 8-10 times before state. This doesn't create a rhythm for the athlete, it forces them to hold on at the end of the season. Create a rhythm that allows certain athletes to cover the big meets, and certain developing athletes to cover varsity when the A team is training. Ask yourself if your top athletes need to run league meets, dual meets, or small invitationals.

You do not have to sit back and play defense all the time as a coach. It is okay to upset other team's rhythms. As you compete against many of the same teams often, you will learn the rhythms and goals of the teams you face. Once you know what they are shooting to do, you can counter their plans. If you know a coach really, really wants to win a key race at a specific invitational, you can stack your team to beat them. You may think "what does that matter," but by beating them there, you are changing their rhythm and the normal success that they use for later on down the line. You can change a team's rhythm by attending a meet you don't normally attend, forcing them to have to compete harder than they want to at a specific point in the season. As you become elite, you will not only look for opportunities for your athletes and team to find their seasonal rhythm, but you will look for ways to throw off the rhythm of the teams you have to beat. You should fear no one, but you will fear even less the teams that you are starting to control.

Remember that you will make mistakes. The key to being "elite" is not that you are perfect, it is making fewer mistakes than your peers do each season. Coaches that recognize the mistakes they make along the way, have a distinct advantage in fixing those errors and keeping them from happening again in the future. Find the rhythm that works for your program and hone the season into a finely tuned machine. At the end of every season, make sure to sit down and identify the adjustments that need to be made for next year's cross country season.

Building a Dynasty: Developing Three Varsity Teams at Once

If you want to build a dynasty, something that doesn't come and go and is a program that is ALWAYS in contention, you have to plan effectively to develop three varsity teams at the same time. You have this year's varsity team, next year's varsity team, and your future varsity team all developing at the same time. That is what makes up our varsity group. The 9th graders in this group that make up the future varsity are still doing the work the other 9th graders are doing, but they are surrounded by and firmly entrenched in the varsity mindset with the other varsity teams.

This year's varsity team is the short term focus. These are the athletes that will be lining up for you in the big invites, league finals, sectionals, state, and Nike Cross Nationals (NXN). This is the win NOW team! You have been bringing them along for a while and they are the athletes that will determine the results for this season. All short term decisions that are made for the team are made with these athletes in mind. Utilize them when needed, otherwise focus on training instead of racing, and developing their rhythm to be ready to deliver when it matters most.

Developing your next year's varsity team is just as important. They are there, hand in hand with the current varsity, learning and preparing to take over next year as many of the older athlete's graduate. These athletes should be utilized in varsity situations to allow the current varsity to rest, which will give them the experience they need to be ready for big races when called upon the following year. These are the athletes that will run sweeps races in meets that we are resting out our top group. They will run in rated or regular varsity races at invites when the current varsity is running the sweepstakes race. Take every opportunity to get this group in the race with something important on the line. Put pressure on them. Teach them. When the current varsity makes a mistake, make sure they learn from it so they don't make that mistake the next year. Your job as an elite coach is to have this team ready to take over as soon as the season ends, so that there is always a top 7 focused and ready to move the team forward.

To me, the most important group you are developing is your future varsity! This group is the group that will determine how good your team is 2-3 years down the road. You can't neglect this group, rather that should get a very large amount of your time. Don't pawn them off on a frosh coach, or leave them training with JV, they need to be with the varsity athletes learning what it takes to be a varsity athlete. You should modify their training for what they are physically ready for, but you need to be molding their minds, forming the bonds together that will come into play in the future, and gaining their trust. As they see you making successful decisions with this year's varsity, they will learn to trust you. They need to be right in the middle of the action, and when you get a chance to run them in big time varsity races, you take it! Find and foster the leadership of this group, they are your future team captains. I call this group our Future State Champions, and program them to be ready when it is their turn on that line.

The most valuable athlete on any cross country team is a fast frosh girl. She has the ability to offer the team 4 varsity seasons, so finding ways to get as many varsity level frosh girls you can each summer is one of the most important things you can do as a coach. Once you get them, your job is to make sure you get them in your future varsity group and develop them to be ready to take over when the time comes. Some will make an immediate impact, so you lose that development time and you will need to use the teachable moments during the season to have them ready.

Be prepared at any moment to part ways with any athlete on your team. Sometimes it just doesn't work out. It may be parent interference, an athlete with a poor work ethic or a bad attitude, or just a kid that has become a cancer to your team.

Every athlete on your team is replaceable. If anyone decides that they are more important than the team, let them know they can be a part of the team and work inside those team goals, or go find something else to do. Build a team culture, and protect it from the cancer that can grow inside of it. We have always called this **addition by subtraction.**

Changing Lives: The Personal Impact You Can Make on Athlete's Long Term

As a head coach, you have the ability to change many lives for the better. Teaching athletes the value of hard work, how to overcome adversity, and how to obtain a goal are things that they will use the rest of their lives. Many of your athletes will idolize you, and many will refer back to your teachings throughout their lives. Never underestimate the power of the words that are coming out of your mouth, good or bad. At Great Oak, we teach our athletes that if they want to be elite, that they have to be more than just a fast runner. We teach them that to be elite they must be a good teammate. They must be respectful to the other teams and fans. We make sure they police their mouths and their actions. And most of all, that they contribute! Everyone contributes in different ways. You can be the person that cheers like crazy every single race! You can be the older athlete that mentors' the younger athletes. You can fundraise a ton for the team, so that we can reach our goals. If you are on our team you will learn to contribute, even if it is as simple as carrying the canopies and chairs to and from the bus, you will bring something to the team. What you will find when you expect more from the athletes than just running, is that they will expect more from themselves and more from each other. Don't be afraid to raise the expectations on your athletes, they can handle anything you throw at them!

It's not about you! This is the phrase that I say the most when trying to teach athletes about what our culture means. Nobody is more *important* than the team, we are all a *part* of the team. Each one of us will make up different aspects of our program each season, but none of us should approach the season as if we are the most important piece. Teaching teenagers that it isn't about them is critical, because as they get good, they will see the results through a bit of a tilted lens. They will see it through the eyes of what they have accomplished and helped accomplish. Your job as a coach is to make sure that you add a filter to that lens, and that filter is to see the whole of the team, before you see what you have done for and with the team. When someone learns to care about the results of the team more than their personal results, they will have learned one of the most important lessons in life. It isn't about what you get, but what you can give. Cross country more than just about any other team teaches this important lesson.

Elite teams have the ability to learn the importance of teamwork and selflessness at a very high level. Coaches should at all times be looking for ways to teach those lessons. Elite teams will be put in very high stress situations. Stress can cause fear, distress, anger, conflict, and a fight or flight reaction in your athletes. True elite teams don't hide from this and they don't believe these things won't happen. Rather, elite coaches know that these things will happen and it is our job to use them as teachable moments, not destructive points on our timeline or road map. I've often diffused many situations by my temperament, but not everyone has a dominant personality. You must find your way to recognize disruptive points on your road map, and utilize the skills that you have to make the needed adjustments. One of the best ways to do this is to teach and establish the program's culture, and to have its foundations based on teamwork and selflessness above other traits. Elite teams can win based on talent in the short term, but to win consistently over the long term, you must find a way to bond your athletes together. That is impossible if individual athletes are more important than the whole.

Teaching respect and sportsmanship is the base of any

elite culture. You can't have athletes that are elite if they aren't elite sportsman. They may be talented, but in our program, you can't reach elite status as an athlete unless you do *everything* well, not just running. In 2019 we suffered a heartbreaking loss to Newbury Park at Nike Cross Nationals by just 4 points on the boys' side. As I stood there devastated for those young men who had given us everything for a chance to be called national champions, I couldn't help but feel a sense of pride as they instinctively and immediately went over and congratulated the Newbury Park team. As devastated as they were in that moment, they didn't let it stop them from being elite. They knew that they needed to show respect to the sport, and give Newbury the respect that they had earned. There is never an easy time to lose a national championship. Seeing our athletes handle it with the class they did left me with the feeling that they had learned what they needed to learn on the journey. Nothing is more important than that.

What would you want your athletes to say about you when you retire? When you hit the end of your coaching journey, what do you want to be known for? Winning championships? Being a fun coach? Being someone who cared? Really sit down and project 25 years into the future and ask yourself what you would want any random athlete to say about you. Once you know who you want to be as a coach, it is easy to coach in a way that will make that happen. It doesn't matter if you win all the time if most of your athletes despise you for it. You have to build a balance and trust with your athletes that they don't see you as a source of stress, rather as a source of inspiration. You need your athletes to see you as a guide down a difficult road, one that can lead them to the goals that they have set. If you do that, your athletes will remember you as an important person in their life. You will never hurt anyone's feelings by letting them know that you care about them.

CHAPTER TWO: FOCUS, DEDICATION, AND DRIVE

One of my biggest strengths as a coach has always been that I will work until the job is finished. It never really mattered how long it took or how hard I had to work, as long as it would make the team better, I was willing to do it. It is that resiliency that defines the success that my teams have had. We may not win every race, but we are competing to win most every race we are in. The athletes in our program learn how to put their heads down and grind, consistently. We know we are a program that works harder than the majority of the programs we will face on the course, and that gives us confidence. It is your job as a head coach to outwork as many of your peers as you can on a consistent basis, so that your team will be the most prepared when it matters the most.

As a younger coach I spent hours running the numbers. What happens if I do this? What happens if we get this athlete out for the team? Can we make the post season if we up the mileage? Oftentimes I would *will* these things into existence. Things don't happen by chance, and often you have to do a lot of pushing to get exactly what you want. To bring the best out of the athletes that you are working with, you consistently need to bring out the best in yourself!

Make a list of your five greatest strengths and your five greatest weaknesses as a head coach. Can you make any of your strengths better? What makes those weaknesses so weak for you as a coach? What can you do to work on them? You will find the best way to fill in your own personal coaching gaps is to identify them, and come up with a plan to develop yourself in those areas. If you struggle with planning practices, then you need to spend 30 minutes more per day planning, research good practice plans, and reach out to other coaches for examples of what they do for their practice planning. Identify your weaknesses, and become focused on eliminating as many of them as possible. Focus on your strengths and identify the steps you can take to make them not only positives in your abilities, but ones that you are so good at that you could mentor others in them. Make time to master your craft!

Coaching Attitude: Your Athletes Will Mirror You!

Intensity! If you ask people around me for one word that describes me, my guess is many would say intensity. I don't consider myself that intense all the time, in fact I'm pretty relaxed and fun loving. When I get into something though, I can go from zero to intense really quickly! That intensity has defined our program, our outcomes, and the perceptions that people outside our program have had of me, our coaching staff, and how our athletes approach the sport. It is very important to understand that your athletes will mirror you and the personality you bring. If you are quiet and have a small personality, it is quite probable that your team will have athletes that work with that type of coach and will show that side of themselves at meets.

Defining a personality that establishes your team and culture is crucial if you want people to follow you. I see coaches all the time that have the title, the kids on their team are happy to be on the team, but they don't really aspire to anything. It is just a chance to hang out, maybe someone runs fast, maybe they don't, but nobody is really worried about it. If you want to be elite, it starts with you and the tone you set. One of the first things I say to my new 9th grade athletes is "you are here to win a state championship." I establish that expectation from the very first moment I'm with them. That is the goal, that is why you are here, and that is the intensity you will get from me as your coach every single day. We will be the best. This isn't a running club where you show up when you want to, that is something you skip when anything else comes up, this is your life. This is a commitment that will change your life. When you program someone like that from day one, they understand what they are getting themselves into and when they buy in, the sky is the limit.

You will show your athletes how to respond to things, so you better have a plan in place on how you want them to act when adversity or a surprise hits. In 2009 our girls missed winning the state title by three points and I did not handle it well. I read the girls the riot act after the race, I told the newspaper I was unhappy with their effort, and was an all-around poor sport. In retrospect, what I realized was that I had only considered the possibility of us winning and wouldn't even think about what happens if we lose. While this works great when you win, it can bring out a side of you that isn't pretty if things don't go the way you expect them to. What I learned was I had to prepare myself for all possible outcomes and how I would respond the adversity if it happened. If I leave it for the moment, then emotion takes over. If I am prepared for all outcomes, then I will respond how I have prepared to respond. Two years later our girls took 7th place and had an all-around bad race at the state meet. This time I was prepared! I built the girls up and thanked them for their hard work. I took responsibility for the loss and went to work preparing the changes that would catapult us to the best program in California history starting in 2012. Instead of emotion and assigning blame, I learned that the head coach always gets the credit for winning and losing and it isn't what happens to you, it is how you respond to it that matters the most.

To win consistently, you better have some form of a big personality. If you don't have a big personality, you better recruit one! Somebody on your coaching staff better be the one that makes your team the place to be. Hire the cool teacher on the staff that everyone loves that knows nothing about cross country. They don't need to be an expert in running, they are already an expert at working with kids and making things fun. Surround yourself with people that fill in the missing pieces of your personality. Everyone can have a role on the team coaching wise, but they can also have a role personality wise as well. Find what you are missing in your program, and discover someone to help you fill in that hole. Turn your weakness into a strength by bringing in someone to be the big personality. It will help you draw and keep athletes in your program and allow you to focus on the things you excel at.

Elite coaches typically have a personality that does not accept failure. Failure may happen, but they are always moving forward, looking for a solution so that the team can reemerge better. Things will happen along the way to greatness, and how a coach handles that makes all the difference in the world. Coaches that freak out over every little thing tend to alienate athletes, parents, and others. Coaches that see every setback as an opportunity to grow will find ways to make their program better. To be an elite coach, you have to want to manage the egos of your top athletes, while motivating the next level crew to close the gap with the top group, while not forgetting about the importance of developing the frosh crew for the future.

Surround Yourself with Great People

Without a doubt, most of the coaches we look back on throughout history didn't accomplish greatness alone. Surround yourself with the people you need to be successful, not the people that think they should be there, but the people YOU want there. Put together a coaching staff of people that truly want to be on your mission.

Hire people who see and believe in your vision, not people who think they know everything about running. You don't want to hire your replacement, you want to hire people that are passionate about the cause, excited to work with kids, accept and want to build the culture, and understand and buy into their role on the team. When assembling a coaching roster, you are looking to hire people that help fill holes for you. In a larger program that can be someone to run your core strength program, someone to work with the frosh group, someone to run the junior varsity group, someone to film or be in charge of social media, and so on. Don't hire people that want to be you because that job is taken, find role players that fill the holes you have in your coaching style, or that take things off your plate to allow you to spend more time coaching the athletes.

Coach Daniel Noble and I began at Great Oak in 2004. We quickly learned to trust each other, and realized that we were on the same mission. Greatness was a requirement; we weren't here to build anything average. Dan's gift, and so few actually have it, is that he is a master at looking at the program as a whole and finding its weaknesses. Year after year he would pick apart not only our results, but what we needed to fix going into the upcoming season so that we could improve and move to the next level. Without Coach Noble, there wouldn't be the Great Oak cross country everyone sees today. His willingness to stay out of the spotlight and be the person behind the scenes who fills in my weaknesses as a coach so that we could improve is why we have become the team we are. He came from baseball, and his tough demeanor as a coach was the perfect yang to my yin. When you are finding assistants, find someone you can trust, find someone that shares your goals and values, and that wants to challenge you to be your best, but doesn't want your job. Don't hire a yes man, hire a coach that you want to share the journey with. There is no doubt in my mind that Daniel Noble is the greatest assistant coach in the nation!

We have had many different assistants through the years.

Some come and go, and some make a commitment to the program and to the athletes. When you get lucky enough to find people that will give up this much of their life to help you succeed, reward them! Get them nice coaching gear, pay them as well as you can, listen to their voice, and give them a piece of the success. Coach Noble built our core and strength program and is always working at ways to make us stronger. Coach Vicki Espinoza retired from our program a few years ago as a champion for the junior varsity athletes on the team. She was a face a voice for athletes that can often be overlooked, and they loved her for it. I was lucky enough to hire Coach Kylie Martin to be our frosh coach after she graduated from college, and she has done an amazing job of indoctrinating the athletes into how we think as a program, and continued our culture of developing athletes. Find people that want to give their time to the athletes, and you will have a great coaching staff. I have been blessed to be surrounded each season by lots of great coaches!

Empower the coaches you hire to develop athletes and to make a difference. You can't coach everyone, and you can't reach everyone. Assistant coaches are there to assist you as the head coach, they are there to fill in the gaps that you have and to help figure out how to better serve the program's needs. You don't hire people because they want to wear the team shirt, you hire people because they are good for kids, and because they can make your program better! If you are hiring someone that doesn't make your program better, you may not want to hire them. Once you have someone in your program, you are responsible for training them and making sure they understand their responsibilities and what you want them to do. Nobody wants to stand there and watch you coach, although sometimes that will be the case. What people want to do is help, they want to engage, and they want to know they are making a difference. Give them specific team responsibilities (fundraising, attendance, core leader, bus scheduler, etc.), as well as athletes that they directly work with. Everyone wants to have a group of athletes they get to coach. You give them the workouts, and they execute your plan. You are not empowering them to replace you, instead you are empowering them to execute the program philosophy and workouts they receive from you. Listen to your assistants and give them a voice. You don't always have to agree or do what they want, but people want to be heard. Ultimately, empowered assistant coaches will be with you a long time, where clipboard holders will come and go. It is up to you to find people that want to help you build the program, and it is up to you to empower them to do just that.

Put in the Time

If you spend one more hour a day for a whole year on improving as a coach, would you improve? I guarantee that you will. Whether it is longer practice times, reading more, or reaching out to other coaches to pick their brains, there are many things you can do to get better as a coach. Don't settle for doing what you did when you were in high school or college as an athlete, instead you have to adapt to the new level of competition and expectation of this generation. Times change and you have to change with them.

To me the first thing any head coach must master is that the job is finished when it is completed. Many coaches don't want to put in 6-10 hours a day working on their teams, so they set them up with short sighted goals and low expectations. You hear this all the time from coaches; "We were done with practice in 45 minutes today" or "I don't care if we win league, we are just focused on having fun." These types of statements by coaches are really saying "I don't want to spend the time that it takes to build a real program, so let's just mess around and have fun and not worry about any of the stresses or pressures that come with the expectations of winning." If you want to be great, you have to outline what it is that your programs are trying to accomplish in the short and long term. What do you see your teams being capable of? What type of time and effort is that going to take from you to build it? Often, I've had people marvel at all we have accomplished in our program, like it just happened out of thin air. They didn't go through the years of parent attacks, athlete's crying because change is hard, administrators that didn't care and weren't supportive. Building an elite team requires YOU to put in more time each day than you want to, and it requires it because you have a choice to be average or to be great. If you choose great, then you stop working when the job is completed.

What does that mean for balance in life? It means there is no balance. Balance is for average people. To be average is to never really push the boundaries, to never challenge yourself or others to be their best. If your goal is to be a great coach, a great parent, a great teacher (or other profession), you will always be frustrated by the fact that something is going to suffer. You don't see great coaches winning teacher of the year award. That time is spent on the field. You have to decide early on as a coach, are you willing to live with an imbalance in your life? Can your spouse live with that imbalance? Can your kids? Instead of looking for a way to balance your life, realize that each part of your life will make sacrifices at specific points of the year. At certain points coaching is pretty much a full time job and much more. At other times, you will have to put everything you have into your own children or your spouse or your job. It is an ever moving target, and you have to manage it, but *do not expect it to be balanced, and do not expect the people in your life to understand it.* If you want to be great, expect to periodically alienate those around you, even when you long to give them your undivided attention. Greatness isn't fair, it is all encompassing. Before you decide to go all in on coaching, understand that lesson.

The early years of my career were a lot easier. I didn't have kids and my wife was out there coaching with me. Our schedules were the same, and that helped a lot. If you are looking to find balance the best you can, look for crossover. Make cross country meets a family affair, where your wife and kids look forward to going to the meets and supporting the team. If you teach, find a way to incorporate your coaching into your teaching day. If you teach science or PE, do lessons that incorporate running. When I was 24, I had a ton of energy and could work for hours. As I've gotten older, I need to be smarter about spending my time on the things that are the most important, and delegating things that I don't want to do any longer. It is ok to hire people to complete some of the things you need to get done, but you need to instill them with the same work ethic that it will take to help the program be great.

In my early years I spent a lot of time running the numbers. Projection after projection to see what we could accomplish as a team. Add in a projected frosh and how do the numbers change? Add in a transfer and how do we stack up? Up the mileage or add a new component and how does the team outlook transform? I spent hours running simulation after simulation to determine how good we could get as a program. What I found was that I would go out and find the athletes that I needed to make my most amazing projections come true. The act of projecting our success forced my competitive nature to find a way to make that success come true. That meant I would identify the key incoming 9th graders and spend a ton of time recruiting them. I would email them, and if that didn't work, I would call them. If a phone call didn't work, I would ask the parents if I could do a home visit, and I would show videos and PowerPoints to the athlete and their parents to try to get them to see my vision. Many came out just because I was so passionate that they wanted to see what all the fuss was about. Ultimately, many of my projections (winning league, winning CIF, winning State, and winning NXN) came true because I projected what it would take and let my competitiveness find the athletes on our campus to make them happen. It is a constant compulsive desire for greatness that drives any coach to spend the time that it takes to be the best in the country.

Where Are You Trying to Get?

Where am I trying to get has been the single most important question in my coaching career! I came to Great Oak to build a program that could compete with anyone in the nation, and understanding that allowed me to build in a very different way than someone who is trying to create a fun place for children to hang out. I wanted to build a program the embodied the very essence of our team moto "World Domination," a program that showed up to meets and everyone else watched them walking in knowing that was THE program. That was the program that set the bar for what a cross country team should be. That concept has driven me to try to hone and perfect each and every aspect of what I do. So, I ask you...Where are you trying to get?

In order to understand where you are trying to get, you must understand why you are doing what you are doing. What is driving you? Why do you want to accomplish your goals as a coach? For me, it has always been simple. I am hypercompetitive, which is really just a fancy way of saying that I like to compete. At everything. Now as I've gotten older, I have learned to temper it somewhat, but at the end of the day I want to compete and I want to win. That drives me to learn how to win, to push myself to be the best in whatever arena I enter. From the moment I got my bearings as a cross country coach, I started thinking about what it would be like to win a state championship. That fueled a fire in me to learn as much as I possibly could about this crazy sport. At the end of the day, this has to be the most basic sport there is, but yet so many coaches have barely scratched the surface on the potential of their team's abilities. Think about your why and where you are trying to get. What approach should you take? Start by outlining the rules you will live by as a coach:

Rules Coach Soles Lives By:

1. *It is all about the kids.*

2. *Surround your athletes with great people.*

3. *Be the hardest working coach you know.*

4. *Be prepared for anything.*

5. *Find a mentor/be a mentor.*

6. *Leave the sport better than you found it.*

7. *Realize that success is right around the corner, but you must keep working for it to happen!*

8. *Patience is never easy, but often worth it.*

9. *If you want it more than your athletes do, the end result won't be what you are hoping for.*

10. *Never quit!*

There are basically two schools of thought on approach. On one hand you have the perfect the process people like Inky Johnson who say, "The process is more important than the product." Master the process and the results will follow. That is contrasted by the intensity of trainer Tim Grover who says, "Crave the result so intensely that the work is irrelevant." So, which is it, process or product? The answer is both, but really you have to figure out which one works for you. Are you a coach that wants to master something thoroughly in hopes that the mastery will lead to success? Or do you believe that if you want an outcome more than anything, you will work to make it happen? Does the end goal drive you or is the process the most important thing? My main goal as a young coach was to build a national class program that would win state and national championships. Those end goals forced me to work at a very high level, consistently, to get the program to a place where I felt it could do just that. I do believe a lot in process mastery, but you must, in an instant, abandon process if you feel it is limiting your chances of hitting your end goal. Figure out what drives you, and which one will help you get where you want to go.

As you set up your road map for any season or program, make sure you shoot for the stars! Where do you want to be in 1 year? 3? 10? True success isn't planned one day at a time, it is planned out many years in advance. Putting together a plan that lays out where you want to be over the course of the time you will be coaching, allows you to map out when and where you are going to be pushing for things and encourages you to find solutions to problems that arise along the way so that you can hit your mark. What is the first major goal your program needs to accomplish? What would be an amazing goal? What is your final destination goal? Spend the time to create a 10-year plan with where you want the program to be mileage wise, team size wise, process wise, and the success you plan to achieve along the way. Update this plan regularly, as it should be ever evolving as you evolve as a coach.

What happens when you get there? Often the hardest part of accomplishing the goal of winning a championship, is starting over to do it again. I have always likened it to a poker tournament. You can't get knocked out at the final table and then immediately jump right into another tournament. The beginning is so different than the end, and you will usually rush the early part of the tournament just trying to get to the end so that you are competing for the big prize again, often overplaying hands and getting knocked out early. We often do this as coaches. We want to just fast forward to state or NXN, give us another chance to win another title. We forget that they success at the end of the season often comes from the patience at the beginning. The truth is though, that the joy of coaching comes from the journey. Mastering the nuances of the new group of athletes, and the challenges of putting different pieces together to get the same results. Remember what got you there the first time. Make adjustments, but lock in the cultural and structural pieces that worked the first time, while still recognizing that YOU must be the one that adapts and changes to fit the new group of athletes. Subtle differences in clientele can give you much different results. You don't want to forget the successes you have had in previous seasons, but you have to start over each year with new goals and a new road map. You know how to win, now build a path to do it again. Take nothing for granted!

CHAPTER THREE: IGNORING THE MINUTIA IN A SEA OF IMPORTANCE

After a couple years of working at Great Oak, I was speaking with one of my assistants about the direction of the program. He had a very different view of where he thought we should be headed, and being twice my age, I always listened to his advice. One of the things he shared with me was that I was not well liked by many of the coaches he had known during his long coaching career. People felt I was cocky, often spoke about things I was too young to know, and that I didn't always come off as a good guy. Now I know the instinct here is to be offended, but the truth was that most of that was probably true. The way I looked at it was that I wasn't out there to make friends, I was out there to **WIN**. I didn't want to just beat other teams, I wanted to "dominate" them at all levels. Nothing is more frustrating to an opponent than to not only lose, but to lose across the board, to not pick up any semblance of success. Killers don't want to beat you, that want to take away any appearance of even a moral victory. That mindset does not make you popular. What it does do is challenge the status quo, the good old boy networks full of average coaches that have been around forever, and forces people to take note. Is this new team and their coach a contender or just a pretender who lucked into some talented kids?

I realize that my personality is different from many that will read this book. We are all very different from each other, but the characteristics it takes to compete against the best coaches in the country year in and year out are all very similar. You better develop thick skin. You will need to learn how to filter through the tremendous amount of information coming your way as a head coach, especially if you are a successful head coach. You are going to have to come to grips with the fact that elite head coaches don't know what the word *balance* means in their life, and most importantly, you have to maintain your agenda and not fall prey to what other's want you to do.

To be truly great at anything you do, you have to be the conductor. You can't let others get in the driver's seat and tell you what should be happening. Pay attention to the motives of others. Many seem to start with good intentions, but often can change sides quickly if they don't feel their voice is heard like they want it to be. Run your show, and find people to support you in that venture.

Lions Don't Lose Sleep Over the Opinions of Sheep

In my fourth year of coaching at Great Oak we began the season at the Buena Park quad meet, which was our opportunity to show that we weren't afraid of anyone. The year prior, we upset Murrieta Valley to win the Inland Empire Championship on the girl's side which was a shock to everyone. In my exuberance in an interview after the meet I uttered that we weren't afraid of anyone and "would take on anyone, anywhere, anytime!" That is a bold statement for a coach that hadn't really ever won anything of significance in a state loaded with talented teams and coaches. Shortly after that Fountain Valley's head coach Barry Migliorini called my bluff and challenged us to come out the next year at Buena Park to take them on and back up my tough talk. After a particularly hot summer going into the meet, needless to say we were well behind where we needed to be to take on a high mileage, well coached program like Fountain

Valley. They destroyed us, leaving no doubt who the better team was. The follow up article on the meet did a lot to highlight my arrogance and how I had gotten ahead of myself, forgetting how great the Orange County teams were. I got calls and emails from friends all over the state asking me if I was upset for such a harsh article. The truth in my mind though was truly that lions don't lose sleep over the opinions of sheep. Nobody can write down who I am. I control that narrative. Anyone can make me look bad short term, but the vision I see in my head each day will occur, and anyone who doubts me will be the one who ultimately looks foolish.

Many people up to this point had doubted me as a coach, but when you see your vision in your head as clear as day, the opinions of others don't matter. The only things that matter are the things that are in your way. People having an opinion about whether I had overreached, been arrogant, or just thought too highly of our chances as a team, didn't understand the vision I saw in my head about what we were about to become. ***Never let people that hold no stake in your vision affect outcomes in your program.***

There is one thing about getting good that nobody tells you. You have to learn it and overcome it, and it can be painful. Once the trolls come out, the doubters, the people that want to make you look selfish or small, then you know you are getting somewhere. If nobody doubts you, especially early on, you probably aren't scaring anyone. To make waves, to create change, you have to scare people. The more you frighten them, the more they will attack you and your program. They will make up lies, spread rumors, talk bad about you to anyone who will listen. This is a natural response for many people when it comes to change, but it is a <u>key identifier for you</u> that you are going in the *right direction*. You are upsetting the apple cart and it is making people nervous. Keep going, put your head down and keep grinding. Don't let others opinions force you to make decisions that are opposite to what you know you need to be doing to continue moving forward. At this point, any press is good press for your program and for you as a coach. Utilize it to put your team on the map.

The Power of Filtering: Learning What to Focus On

One of the biggest mistakes I see coaches make is not learning to filter out what is important to your vision, and what is just noise. Teachers may get 50 or more emails a day about all sorts of things. You do not have to answer, read, or respond to all of this! Identify the items you need to respond to, and the items that are just daily or weekly items that everyone gets that you can ignore. Identify where you need to spend your time, and ignore the people that are just talking to hear themselves talk.

There is a great scene in the movie *Moneyball* where Peter Brand is watching a game on TV and the announcers give credit to the manager for the A's winning 7 games in a row. Peter turns to Billy Beane and asks him "Did you hear that?" Billy responds, "I heard 7 in a row." This scene illustrates exactly what you need to do as a coach to filter the information that is swirling around you. Media, parents, administration, athletes, other teams doing well or not doing well. There is a lot to take in each day. Your job is to focus on what you need to hear and process, not what everyone around you wants you to hear. You can't solve all the problems for the other teachers in your department, and you shouldn't even try. What information that comes in during the day do you need to learn to avoid? What emails should be going straight to your trash bin without being opened? You have a lot to accomplish, and to do that you can't read every email, answer every phone call, and be there for every little thing that comes up. You have to triage it, and focus on the critical pieces that must be addressed to make your team better. The other items are often just noise. If focusing on your team is down the list for you, expect the results to finish down the list as well.

Often you have to filter with your athletes to get to the point. Youth, fear, inexperience, and emotions all can cloud the message that an athlete is trying to share. Being able to filter through those things to find the actual message is critical if you want to hear your athletes. I've often found that I have to filter out the opinions of their parents or their friends before I can actually hear what they want to tell me. Usually when a 16-year-old wants to talk to me and they have a very rehearsed spiel that sounds like someone told them to say it instead of something they are feeling, it almost always is coming from the parents. You have to learn to filter out what they are being told versus what they actually feel or need.

Your focus should be on your team. Everything else is secondary to that. Once that is not the case, your results will show that you spent your time somewhere else. Many of us are busy with other jobs, and that is understandable. Utilize the time that you have during your day to make your team better. You can't show up at the start of practice and have that be the first time you thought about what needs to be done that day. Show up prepared and ready to put your vision into action.

Managing Other Commitments

On the wall right before you enter my home office, I have a small framed wall poster that offers 21 Suggestions for Success by H. Jackson Brown Jr. that I often read. I don't remember when we got it, it is just one of those things that has just always seemed to be around. Rule number one on that list of recommendations is "Marry the right person. This one decision will determine 90% of your happiness or misery." This couldn't be truer when it comes to being married and coaching! Your happiness as a coach will often be defined by the understanding of your spouse and what they understand your responsibilities to be, but even more so what they know you must do to be successful. Don't take your spouse for granted! Include them, shield them, and understand that from time to time your lack of availability for family will frustrate them.

I have been blessed with a wife that was a great competitor on the track, and who also has been an assistant and head coach in cross country and track. She is acutely aware of what it takes to be successful in the sport, which allows me to talk to her about all of the things our team is going through. Instead of it annoying her, she loves to be a part of what I'm doing, and she is my ultimate confidant. She doesn't always see my side of it, but she does point out all the sides to what is going on. No matter how frustrating that can be, she is always there to challenge me to be my best. She does a great job of reminding me that date night is not a time to talk coaching, a point we all need to remember to keep a healthy relationship.

Unfortunately, not everyone is as lucky as I am when it comes to marrying someone that understands the demands and passions coaching brings. My wife Teresa ran track from elementary school through college, and enjoys coaching when she can. She has stepped away from teaching and coaching to raise our children, but the understanding is there. The patience with what I'm wrestling with is there. I've seen plenty of coaches get divorced, and most of the time it comes down to the fact that the spouse doesn't understand the passion that their significant other has for their coaching. Communication is the key. If this is important to you, make sure that they know it. If you have goals, make sure that they know them too. At the end of the day, they are on this journey with you, and you better sit down and make sure everyone is on the same page. My wife knows there will be times where I'm available, and times I'm not. Times I come home hot and angry, and times I come home devastated. She is ready for it, because she is bought into the journey. She is bought into that journey with me, not against me. Make sure you have that conversation before you go all in, or you may end up going all in by yourself.

True management comes from understanding that sometimes you have a lot of time to be a father/mother, sometimes you are 100% focused on coaching, and sometimes your priority is being a spouse. There is give and take, and it doesn't happen all at once, so you have to make sure everyone understands what mode you are in for it to work, otherwise jealousy and frustration will take over and ruin it. To be elite, there will be no balance in this. Don't try for balance, try to be the best you when you are in whichever mode you are in at the time, knowing that sometimes you will be an awful parent or spouse, but you will make up for it when your time opens back up. If you don't make up for it, then you will run into problems. Eliminate anything that is not needed. I see coaches that are more worried about having some brews and hanging out with their bros then spending that spare time with family. Guess what, college is over. Sacrifice everything that can be sacrificed to take your coaching to the next level.

Don't Get Caught Up in Other People's Agendas

Every person you run into has an agenda. Some agendas are small, some are big, some don't matter, and some are going to conflict with you on a daily basis. As a head coach you have to try to figure out what your agenda is and eliminate the worrying about what other people's agendas are. Do not let people spread their craziness in your head!

One of the big agendas you have to avoid is the activities director on your campus. I don't say this because they are evil people, quite the contrary. Many are amazing at getting kids involved in doing all sorts of things on campus. They may send you 10 emails a day asking for you to do this or support that, or to help with something specific. At the end of the day, an elite coach does not have the inclination to waste their precious time on someone else's agenda. There are probably a few things you need to do in the year with the activity director, so don't waste your time answering emails and setting up things for this aspect of the school. You have many more important things to do! Let the teachers on campus that are not coaching put their extra time into assemblies and dance activities. You are not available for these items.

I have been blessed to have worked with many great parents in my program over the years, and most just want to see their kids excel. All parents have an agenda, and usually it is very "their athlete" centric, but sometimes it is about them and they want to help so that they can get the attention or the accolades inside of the team. Make sure when you include parents in your "in group" that you select ones that care about the entire team, and not just their little slice of it.

The Administration's agenda usually comes down to one thing, safety. Now this is one you better pay attention to, because it will get you fired faster than just about anything else. Build your program around keeping athletes safe and you won't have too many issues with your admin. Remember that administrations change over faster than teachers and coaches, so if someone comes in with a tough agenda for your program, realize it won't be that way forever. Build relationships with your admin, and build trust. When they know they can trust you, then they don't have to worry about what you are doing. They have limited time, and they don't want to spend it on someone who is always doing things right. Make good decisions, and keep the admin out of your hair. My biggest goal with admin is to make their job easier, so they aren't trying to be involved in making decisions in my program. I always say one thing about administrations, they don't care about your program the way that you do, so don't expect them to make good decisions for you. Guide them, show them, and teach them what they should care about so that they get to be a fan of your program, instead of detractor.

Head Games – How to Control People's Actions Outside of Your Program

The coaches that have the ability to sway the actions of those not in their program truly have mastered the art of control. Whether through the media, social media, or just the opinions of others, the truly elite coaches in the country have found ways to control the narrative, be it for a specific race or event to the point that other coaches, parents, athletes, or media make decisions based on the information those elite coaches release.

To me, controlling the media is an essential way to make sure that you get fair coverage for your program. Do not let the media write untruths, favor other programs over yours if you are more deserving, or simply get away with lack of coverage. Be polite, but be direct with the media that this is how it is going to go. You run the show, you will let them know what you want out and what you don't, and you control what is shared. If they don't want to give you good coverage, don't let them cover your team. No quotes, no interviews, no talking to athletes. They get access through you. Make sure they do a good job of covering your team fairly, or they don't get to.

There are lots of ways we as coaches can control other head coaches' decisions and game plans. Allowing other coaches to know your plan can force them to create a game plan to stop you or try to beat you. Letting everyone know what you plan to do gives you the ability to intimidate, change course and throw them off, or just get a feel for how the plan is received by other coaches out there to determine if changes need to be made. In the 2015 Track & Field season, we planned to win the 4x1600 relay at Arcadia, which is not easy to do. The meet is one of the most competitive meets of the year and draws top talent and teams from across the US and beyond. We knew that year would come down to us versus Desert Vista from Arizona, coached by the amazing Dr. Jeff Messer. We knew it would be a battle! I ran through every possible scenario to try to formulate a plan that would give us a chance to win. We always ran into one problem... Dani Jones was their anchor and arguably the best miler in the country at the time. I called Destiny Collins and asked her if she would be ok switching in to be the starter, with a goal of trying to open up a 100m lead on the field to force the other legs from Desert Vista and Saugus to run too hard early and not have enough left in the final laps to run us down. She agreed. As we set our plan in motion, it became obvious that we didn't want anyone to really know what was going on, so just Coach Noble, myself, and the four girls were aware of the plan to switch. The head games that we played through media and social media was to build up the matchup between Destiny Collins and Dani Jones. We got everyone psyched up about our lineup, our race plan, and how we thought we were going to win by using the published line up and how the matchup should unfold. Everyone thought they knew what we were going to do.

Meet day arrived and we anxiously warmed up. As they began taking the girls out to the starting line, Sydney Belus who had become a solid sub five minute miler for our team went out as advertised. At the last possible second, we switched Destiny Collins in for Sydney, leaving Sydney to run the anchor leg against Dani Jones. Our parents were so surprised that I believe a few of them were cussing me out in the stands...let's just say they were shocked. Destiny was out like a shot! She instantly built a big lead, and continued to pour it on lap after lap. She finished a good 80+ meters ahead of second place and forced everyone on the other teams to chase us hard. Leg after leg our competitors would get the baton and close on us the first lap, only to give most of it back by the end of lap four. Kiyena

Beatty ran an amazing 2nd Leg, Evelyn Mandel a very good 3rd leg, and when Sydney got the baton, we were still quite a bit ahead. There was just one problem. Dani Jones. Lap after lap Dani closed on our lead. With 200m to go she was right behind Sydney. I wondered if I had made a mistake, if Dani was just too formidable to beat? She has an amazing kick and Sydney was just learning how to race at a high end varsity level. What a tough spot for Sydney to be in. With 150m to go they were neck and neck, in a dead sprint for the finish line. Fortunately, the plan had worked to perfection, and Dani had to spend most of her energy to catch up and didn't have quite enough left to overtake Sydney's kick. Our team had pulled off the upset and the plan had worked! Sydney said when she finished, she was a bit shellshocked and wasn't even sure if we had won. This was a tough spot for a developing athlete, but one that allowed her to prove herself. Never be afraid to give athletes a shot at the big time, and never be afraid to play head games. Sometimes it takes more than just lining athletes up to pull off a victory. Be willing to put on the moves from time to time, and be aware that someone might be doing just that to you.

One of the best mind games you can play, is controlling the decisions of parents and athletes on other teams. Now I know you are thinking, how do I do that and why would I want to? The truth is the psyche of both parents and athletes can often determine outcomes in races. The more a parent or athlete panics, the less confident they will be in their race. The easiest way to do this is to spread disinformation from your athletes to their athletes. Give your athletes things that you know will get back to your competitors or their coaches via social media or another outlet. Often finding out information can upset the race plans or confidence of the team you need to beat. This isn't something you should use often, but there are times you need to move the mathematical needle in your direction just enough to get the win. Like a professional poker player sitting down to win money, sometimes you will have to bluff to win the pot.

Remember that YOU run the show! Your decisions will ultimately lead to the majority of outcomes that your program produces year in and year out. Don't be afraid to be aggressive, or control the narrative in the media, or throw a little disinformation out there to play some head games. You are the single most important long term piece in your program. What you chose to do each day with your team will determine where you end up. Don't be afraid to lead from the front and go after the impossible!

CHAPTER FOUR: ADVERSITY AND LOSING: WHAT WE LEARN AND HOW WE ADAPT

When you are great, everyone wants to see you fall! I remember watching the distance medley relay at Arcadia where our team had a pretty solid lead going into the anchor with Solomon Fountain getting the baton. Solomon was a very consistent runner for us and we knew we would get a 4:10 to 4:13 range out of him on the leg. Truthfully, I felt it was pretty much a wrap at that point, but the anchor leg for Bellarmine was a big strong 800 kid who didn't get the memo that I was confident we would win. Each lap the athlete from Bellarmine was closing and our lead slowly evaporated, and although Solomon had a very good kick, this guy was not going to be denied if he got close enough. I remember standing there and becoming acutely aware that every single coach around me, every one, was cheering hard for Bellarmine. My focus switched from the race to asking myself why all of these coaches from so many different schools were so interested in seeing this team run us down? The truth of course wasn't that they wanted Bellarmine to win, it was that they wanted to see us lose! When you get to the top everyone is gunning for you. Be prepared to take everyone's best shot!

I always tell my kids we either win or we learn. We certainly learned in that DMR that Bellarmine wanted that race more than we did. When you are often successful, it is very easy to cruise when you should be going for the jugular. In that situation, the stadium wanted us to lose more than we wanted to win and it showed. We ran a good race, but when things don't go your way as a coach you have to know each one of your athletes and what you need to say to them to get them to come back stronger in the future. There is always another race!

Adversity: Turning it Into an Asset

Adversity is the most powerful tool you have access to, use it when you get it! Learn from it when it is teaching you something! This generation of parents has taken adversity away from their children and tried to protect them from the harsh realities that life has waiting for them. The reality is that adversity allows us to truly decide how badly we want something and how much we are willing to do to achieve it. Don't shield your athletes from adversity, utilize it to make them stronger.

In 2014 our boys team was ranked in the top 10 nationally a lot of the season. We had lots of talented weapons in our top 7 and at any point in time we knew we could compete with the best teams in the nation. We were the best team in California that season going into the state meet in my opinion, and I believe we were the best team coming out of that meet as well. Cross country in California has 5 divisions and at the end of the divisional state meet all of the athletes are added together and NXN teams are selected through a merge, not direct competition. Although we won our first boys state title against a loaded Division 1 field, we ended up fourth in the merge and were not selected by the committee to attend NXN that year. We were all furious! The teams that were selected ran early in the morning on a very warm day, where we ran in the heat with sun overhead. We had beaten those teams throughout the season and knew we should have made that trip!

That adversity led our 2015 boys team, which returned 5 of the top 7, and was motivated to destroy every team we faced that season. I didn't have to help them develop a reason or a chip on their shoulder, if anything I had to hold them back. Someone had taken something from them, and they knew it. It is one thing to miss out on an opportunity, it is another when you feel deep down in your soul that you were wronged. This group of young men knew who they were, what they wanted to accomplish, and they dared anyone to try to stand in their way! They bulldozed through the beginning of the season, only being tripped up once by a small margin at the Bob Firman Invitational in Idaho by 2 points. Two of the top five from NXN didn't make the trip, which left us a bit short handed. It was definitely a tough loss, but one we learned from.

After losing that meet, the boys promised each other they were not going to lose again that season. It wasn't a coaching move or speech, it was a group of young men who had decided that they were going to perform for each other when it mattered, and they did. They came back a few weeks later and broke the course record at THE course in Southern California, the prestigious Mt. San Antonio College (Mt. SAC) Invitational. They held off an amazing Dana Hills squad at CIF Southern Section Finals and State, and prepared for Nike Cross Nationals. When we got to meet day, the boys warmed up and came in for the final words from the coaches.

We circled up and we shared our thoughts. The boys looked at us and said "Don't worry coaches, we got this." It wasn't a promise or a hope, it wasn't being said because they wanted to win, it was different. It was said in a way that let everyone in our group know that the adversity that we all went through in 2014, was going to be the anger, the hate, the revenge, the fuel to push them to the finish line. And it did.

Using Failure as Fuel

Missing NXN in 2014 gave us all the adversity we needed to dial in and focus on winning in 2015. Our boys were 100% bought in to winning nationals and had a chip on their shoulders the entire season, it was us against the world. Those teams are very hard to beat, because deep down they know they what should have happened and they won't let anything or anyone get in their way again. Our leader that year was Isaac Cortes. He wasn't the fastest cross country runner on the team, but he was the bridge between all of the personalities on the team and could get everyone to rally around the same ideals. He led us to many wins, many course records, and many confidence boosting moments throughout the regular season. He was a very talented middle distance runner, running a 4:06 for the 1600 as a junior. He had higher goals and aspirations, and felt like he could be the top guy on the cross country team, and this was a constant source of frustration for him. I sat down with him and explained to him that we didn't need him to take risks to get an individual win, we needed him to be the best #3 in the country, because that would almost assure that we would win as a team. Set aside the ego and just be the best version of you each time out and we will have the best top three in the country. Now most athletes at his level might have been offended or felt like their coach was holding them back. Not Isaac. Team first all the way, he checked his ego and focused on producing top level performances for his teammates. He dealt with the adversity and frustration of 2014 by sacrificing his personal performances so the team could win. He played it safe, played his role, and pretty much ensured us a victory at Nike Cross Nationals. Give your athletes a chance to lead, to sacrifice, and to believe, and most usually will. Isaac wanted to his teammates to win more than he wanted to be the top guy on the team.

As a coach, take note of the pain caused by failure. It is an opportunity to push those athletes to the next level. Destiny Collins fell at track state as a frosh and as a soph. In those moments I told her to hold onto that pain, to save it, to be ready to use it her junior year. When she got to state her junior track season, she was outkicked in the 1600 and held on for a 4:41 third place finish. She was in tears, devastated at losing a race she so badly wanted to prove herself in. She had another chance in the 3200. When I went to talk with her, she was crying and emotional and frustrated. I told her to remember that pain from her frosh and soph years, that she needed to use it to power herself in the 3200 against an amazing runner in Davis' Fiona O'Keefe. She had to decide before stepping on the track that she was going to win. If she couldn't do that, then she didn't even need to race. She dried her eyes, she said she was running to win, and win she did. She executed the race plan to perfection, sitting on Fiona for the first 2900 meters, and then unleashing an all-out assault with 300 meters to go. She won going away, in 9:53 and proved she could be a state champion in California! All that pain from falling the previous seasons was the fuel that powered her in the middle of the race when Fiona was surging. She doubted herself at times, but when doubt crept in, she thought about those falls, and not allowing another race to slip away. Her win is one of the best State Meet performances in girls' 3200 history. Find your athlete's fuel, and unleash it when they need it the most.

Devastation

The most painful loss I've ever experienced as a coach happened in 2009. We had built a loaded girls' team and we were the favorites to win our first state championship. I was as nervous that week as I have ever been as a coach, I could taste the victory our ladies were about to achieve and race day couldn't arrive fast enough. Now we knew that Torrey Pines had a formidable top three, but we felt like we could put in a gap at the 4-5 range that they just couldn't overcome. Our girls were fit, and we knew there wasn't anyone in our division could match that fitness. Unfortunately, as a coach we don't always see clearly until after a loss. After our hearts are ripped out of our chests and the victory goes to someone else. In this race, I would come to find out that I had prepared our team to a very high level of fitness, but had failed to realize how tired they were from their school workload in the IB program, once we got to the week off from school that we had for Thanksgiving week, four of my top seven just shut down. It wasn't the girl's fault, they wanted it. They tried to seal the deal on race day, including a furious close the last mile to almost win, but they had turned off their focus and it showed badly on race day. Torrey put their top three girls in the top ten and they were able to hold us off by 3 points. 3 points! We were devastated. There are so many places that we could have made up those points, but once the race is over, you can't fix it. You learn from it and come back stronger.

I can honestly say that I didn't smile much for the next six months. How in the world were we going to evolve in 2010 so that this didn't happen again? How could I identify every single issue that led to us losing that state title? How could I fix it? I had to go through it. I had to feel every moment of that despair, to understand that the only fix was **me doing a better job**. Working harder. Doing more. Prepping my athletes better, and getting them to believe they were a state championship team. Often as a championship coach, that devastation, that feeling of despair is what you are working hard to prevent. It is less about winning, and more about making sure you don't have to feel that way again. As you begin to win consistently, you learn that it is really about making sure that your athletes don't have to feel like you did. Adversity is the best teacher, but once you have learned that lesson, you will do everything in your power to avoid the thing that causes that pain.

Now I know what you are thinking. Devastation? Despair? This guy is a little overly dramatic, isn't he? It really depends on how badly you want something. How much of your soul you are willing to give up to make something happen? If you don't really care if you win league, sectionals, state, or NXN, then yeah, it probably seems a little silly. But if you spend almost every waking moment trying to figure out how to make those things happen, it is devastating when you fail. It leaves you with a pit in your stomach that won't go away. I can't tell you every race we have won, or even all the races we have gone to over the years. I can tell you in great detail every time we have lost when we should have won. If you don't feel devastated at a 2nd place finish at the state meet, you never set winning on a high enough pedestal. I always say that 2nd place is an amazing feeling if you were projected to take 7th. If you were projected to win, it is one of the most painful things you will experience as a coach.

Take that pain, that devastation, that despair, and put it to use. It won't go away, at least not for quite a while. Not a day goes by that I don't feel that loss in 2009. That I don't think about the one girl on that team that was a senior, and how she didn't get to stand on the podium with the girls in 2010. That loss drives me, it focuses me, and it reminds me why I must be at my best. It reminds me why I can't get complacent, and why I can't feel satisfied with all of the success we have had. Once I do, I will put another girl or boy in that situation. I will allow them to lose, because I didn't give them my all. If you could take away all of your pain from your life, would you? Our pain, whether for good or bad, is a driving force forward for many of us. Use your pain and put it into developing a championship mindset for your team.

Making Adjustments

What is the difference between the art of cross country coaching and the science? Often, the coaches we consider the best artists of the sport are the ones that make the best adjustments. They take in the information they get from their athletes, the workouts, the meets, the parents, the media, social media, their assistants and team captains, and they utilize it to make key adjustments that lead to the amazing results we see on the course. The better you are as a coach at assessing all of this information, and in turn using it to make adjustments, the better off your athletes will be on race day. To have them be prepared for all they will face when they are in a race situation, it helps to know if the course has changed or has different conditions, this or that team isn't going to attend the meet this year, or that the fastest athlete for your chief competitor is injured or sick. It is your job as the head coach to not only pay attention to this information, but to search it out. A poker player sitting at a table is constantly looking for the information being provided to them by the other players at the table. So are you! To develop a race plan, you need to take all of the information you are getting from every possible source, and make adjustments to your plan as new information comes in.

Elite coaches often make subtle adjustments. Most so small that nobody even notices them. This can be in practice, at a meet, or just in the information passed on to others. A subtle adjustment can be as simple as walking through a race plan with one of your varsity athletes and asking them to push a little harder at a specific point in a race to see if that will help them finish in a better place. Most people watching will never know the adjustment is made, but the coach will slowly but surely make hundreds or thousands of these adjustments over the course of a season to try to hone each athlete and have them ready for their best performances when it matters most to the team. Often, these little adjustments give your athletes the ability to try something new without having to fear failure. I often tell my athletes that if they win, that is on them, but if they lose, then it is on me. Hard not to have confidence when your coach allows you to go out and try out many different race strategies and adjustments to your racing, without having the fear that they will be upset with you if things don't go well. Make adjustments, but take responsibility for those alterations good or bad.

Changing your course strategy for a specific course is

something that takes time and races. We all race many different venues, but no matter where you are, there are the magic courses that everyone holds at a very high level of esteem. That course in Southern California is the Mt. San Antonio College or Mt. SAC course. Although a little shorter than 3 miles, this course is known for its 3 hills, admirably known as Switchbacks, Poop Out, and Reservoir. These hills are known for eating the unprepared for breakfast, and spitting the remains out on the other side of one of the hills! In my early years as a coach, Mt. SAC posed many problems for me. In 2006, our girls' team was entered in the Mt. SAC Invitational Team Sweepstakes race. We proceeded to take dead last. I had to figure out how to prepare my athletes better so that didn't happen in the future! How do I prepare athletes for a course that is so unique and so difficult, that many athletes are going to struggle there? The first thing I did as a coach was take away the mystique. The athletes feared the legendary nature of the course, I had to make it normal for us to eliminate the fear my athletes had of it. Fear leads to uncertain outcomes, and I wanted my athletes to be fearless when it came to this course. I often tell my athletes that you will never fear taking a test that you already know the answers to. My job as a coach was to make Mt. SAC a course that they felt like they already knew how to beat. The second thing I did was add a Mt. SAC workout day to our schedule, so that our athletes felt that we were doing everything we needed to be doing to be prepared for that specific course. Lots of hill sprints, and lots of mileage in and around hills. We made running hills normal instead of scary. We added in athletic movements to our training like box jumps, speed ladders, and HIITS to make sure our athletes could expend large amounts of energy, and keep going. We made Mt. SAC normal instead of scary.

The mental side of adjusting our athletes to be better prepared for the Mt. SAC course was just as important if not more than the physical. We focused on teaching the course in a way that they understood when to push, when to relax, and how and when to take a bit of a mental break during the race. To do this we needed to understand the best philosophy for running a successful race at Mt. SAC. The find this, I watched every Mt. SAC sweepstakes video I could get my hands on. Not only did I watch them, I watched them over and over again, focusing on a different team each time. How did they go out? Did they make a move? How did the teams that went out fast do at the end and overall? How did the teams that went out slow do? What were the common characteristics of the winning teams for the sweepstakes races, year in and year out? What I found was that the teams that went out too fast in the first mile, didn't finish very well and rarely won. Teams that hammered the uphills rarely won. Teams that started too far back tended to finish in the back. So, what was the race plan that has led us to the Mt. SAC team time records, and many consecutive teams sweeps championships? It was simple. We run a controlled first mile, focusing on position and controlled effort. We move up a little going up the Switchbacks, and then hammer the long downhill coming off of the backside of Switchbacks. When we get to the Crossover, we identify who we need to move up to get to and try to maintain a consistent effort up Poop Out. On the backside of Poop Out, we surge down the hill and try to put ourselves in striking distance of the athletes we need to beat. We try to remain strong going up Reservoir, and once we hit the top we push as hard as we can for the final 800 meters or so to the finish line. This race plan has helped us not only win and set records, but has allowed us to take the fear our athletes had of the course out and replace it with a preparation and race plan that ensures they have the best chance to win. In the early years, our teams would often go out way too hard and fade. Now, our athletes know they can relax and have the course come to them by pushing at the right times, and relaxing at specific points along the way. When you identify the key courses for your program, you must study them, test them, and make the adjustments necessary to master them so that your athletes can run their best races each time out. In 2012, our girls team won their first

Grand Sweepstakes Championship at the Mt. SAC Invitational and have gone on to win many more. That last place finish in 2006 was critical in our long term success. Use the mistakes you make as a coach as a catalyst to find the information you need to improve your team each season. The only mistake is not identifying or utilizing the information you find along the way.

Practice adjustments are the most common ones we all make, but many can be critical, playing a huge role in the final outcome of our season. Whether it is adding in a component, taking one out, cutting out a rep or adding some in, or just shutting down a workout that you feel is done well enough, be ready and willing to make adjustments in your training plan on the fly as needed. A large part of coaching is recognizing when things are working and when they aren't. When an athlete needs more, or when they have had enough. Be willing to alter anything you have created, because creation isn't finality, it is possibility. Create unlimited possibilities in your program by being fluid and open to change.

Motivation

Be careful of selling your team logic, most people spend all their time and money on emotions. Learn to tap into the emotions of your athletes, understand what drives them.

When you need to do it the most, you need to be able to delve into that bag of emotional tricks and sell them what they need to hear, when they need to hear it. If you know something particularly motivating about an athlete, save it. Use it when you need it most, use it when they need it most. Find a way to activate that part of them that they might not be able to reach themselves, that part that needs someone saying it to them for it to ignite. As a head coach, you are the instigator of all things, you are the one that makes it all come together. Learn your athletes, and sell them on what they need to hear to be champions.

What does it take to get you to the next level of motivation? What does it take to get your athletes there?

Everyone is motivated by something different, but your team should be motivated by the team goals and the journey you will take together. Identify the items that motivate your team for that season. Beating a specific team, making it to another level than you have ever made before, or just having a fun season together can all be motivation. You will need to identify what motivates your team as a whole, your athletes as individual moving parts of that team, and your coaching staff as the season progresses so that you know which buttons to push as the championship meets approach. I often remind my athletes of the motivational factors that we have for our season while at practice. I want them fired up, ready to perform and go after it. I want our athletes motivated to destroy their opponents when they are given the chance, and I program that in a little each day.

One of the easiest ways to motivate your athletes is to make it personal. Your team wants something, and this team or this individual is blocking you from getting it. They are stopping you from achieving what you want. They are the bad guy! Not really, but to bring out the best in your athletes, you may need to make sure they can identify who they are trying to beat, and why they are trying to beat them. If you have to throw in a few remarks about how they **don't respect us**, or **they think they are better than you guys are**, then that might be the right motivation for your group. You can only go to this well so many times, so make sure to use it when it matters most.

To me, the easiest motivational trick in the book is the **ego**. We all see ourselves at a certain level, and when that is challenged by someone it can ignite a self-worth firestorm that can push an athlete or a coach to do things beyond what they can normally do. When I know I have an athlete battling someone from another team for a potential championship, I love to tell them things like "I've heard he laughs at you, thinks you aren't on his level." Some kids won't care and move on, but some can't check their ego. They become Marty McFly when someone calls him "chicken" and they have to defend their honor. Now this is probably the oldest coaching trick in the book, but if you need to find a way to get a little extra out of one of your athletes, this usually works.

If you have an athlete that has suffered a tragedy in their life, and they have come back stronger, that can be a great motivational point for you as a coach working with them. Sometimes just thinking about all they have gone through will give them the courage they need to face the challenges that lie ahead. Your job is to do it in a way that builds them up, empowers them, and allows them to use their past for strength in their future. Form a bond with the athlete around this aspect of their life that is unique to them, and foster success from that pain. It is amazing how we can look fear directly in the face when it pales in comparison to something, we have already experienced.

Illness and Injuries

The most frustrating thing about distance running is that the very thing that it takes to be great, running a lot, is also one of the things that ups your chance of injury. You can't set goals to win State or NXN, and then say we are only running 25 miles a week and are going to focus on keeping everyone healthy. To be champions, you will have to take some risks along the way. I often liken it to a poker tournament. Sometimes you need to play tight and fold every hand, but sometimes you have to push the action and try to make a move to the next level or you won't make it. In a defined season, there are times where you must take chances. High school cross country has a very defined timeline, so you will need to balance those risks of when to take chances with when you need to be healthy and running your best. An extremely loaded squad may require less hard training, and more focus on staying healthy. A team with less talent and lots of heart, may need to take more risks in training to get to the finish line first. Determine what you have and how you need to adjust that season to have that specific group ready come championship time.

No matter how big your team is, how careful you are as a coach, or how many miles you run, you will always have injuries on your team. Often injuries occur because the athlete has a physical issue that you are not aware of, and the more they push, the greater the chance that issue becomes an injury. Unfortunately, a lot of the time we find out our athletes are having an issue **AFTER** it is too late to shut them down and fix it. Make sure to build in a dialog with all of your athletes so they know what is soreness, what is hurting, and what is a full blown injury. When they can tell the difference, you can guide them on solutions. Some things you have to run through and work out, some things you have to cross train on, and some injuries you just have to rest and let the body heal.

Get your athletes in the right pair of shoes and have them tested to make sure those shoes work for their body. Many running stores or physical therapists can do foot strike tests to see if they pronate or supinate when they run. Putting your athlete in the right pair of shoes can solve a lot of foot strike issues that can lead to much bigger issues later on down the road. Once an athlete finds a style of shoes that works for them, keep them in them! Often shoe inserts or orthotics can be very helpful for athletes that struggle to stay healthy. Find someone to send your athletes to so they can get tested for what will help them the most.

One of the things that I believe is very important for longer mileage is for athletes to wear heavy training shoes with as much padding and protection as possible. It is ok to have lighter shoes for a tempo or fartlek, but for mid to longer runs I want my athletes wearing shoes that offer as much shock absorption as possible to help prevent stress injuries from repeated pounding. Focus on energy absorption and support for longer runs. Stay away from lighter, less supportive shoes when doing longer aerobic running.

Get the flu shot! One of the worst feelings for the athlete and the team is to have an athlete get sick right before a championship meet. I highly encourage every coach to break down with their group what vaccinations that should be getting during the season to try to ensure they won't end up with the flu or worse when they are needed the most. Vitamin supplements can be very helpful for keeping athletes healthy, as many do not eat a healthy enough diet to get all of the Vitamin D or Zinc they need.

There isn't much that I believe an athlete should miss practice for, but I do recommend all coaches keep sick kids home from practice. If they aren't feeling well, they just let me know and tell them I hope they feel better and send them home. The earlier you catch an illness on your team, the better the chance you can slow the spread. Eventually, most kids will catch something, but you don't want them all sick at the same time. If an athlete is injured, I want them at practice doing strength work and remaining a part of the team environment. If not, a lot of fake injuries pop up so kids can take a couple days off to go home and play video games. That doesn't work for building a championship team.

Failing to Hit Your Goals...and Coming Back Stronger

Bouncing back after a tough loss is not easy. In the 2019 cross country season, our boys were ranked number 1 in the nation by many of the media outlets. The truth is we probably were the best team in the country at that point, with tons of talent in our top 7 and a "B" team that was good enough to win our sectional title later in the year. We had experience, confidence, talent, health, and a focus on winning the big one unlike anything we had seen since our 2015 national championship team. Now we knew that Newbury Park was going to be good, but they had not proved that they were going to be deep enough to take us down when it mattered and we felt like we could beat anyone in the nation. When we got to Woodbridge, it was a weird situation, as I had to fly to Oregon to receive an award at my high school. This was something I had promised my high school coach that I would attend, and knowing our team was in the very capable hands of Coach Daniel Noble, I wasn't too worried about it. We knew that Newbury Park would come out guns blazing, and that they would most likely go 1-2 in the race. We felt like our top guys were going to be able to put in a big pack in between their #2 guy and the rest of their athletes. We were excited for the race. A couple things showed that night. One is that I bring a bit of calming and reassurance to the varsity teams that wasn't there with me being gone, and the other was the adjustments I had made for training for Nike Cross Nationals over early season meets had left us vulnerable on a super flat and fast course. Newbury blitzed us, and we weren't ready to respond. That was on me.

We lost to Newbury Park by a score of 36-69, which is a pretty good butt kicking. When I broke down the scores, I learned that Mateo Joseph had fallen hard at the start and ended up pretty much out of it scoring wise for us. Also, two of our other top guys had off nights and weren't anywhere close to what they were capable of. I chalked it up to an off race and figured it would change quickly by the time we got to the Clovis Invite and a rematch later in the season.

Keep calm and refocus. When I returned to school and team practice that following Monday, one of the first things I did was bring in my varsity boys team and asked them "Do I look worried?"

I had that confident smile that you see from someone that knows they are about to kick your butt at something. The boys relaxed and listened, breathing a sigh of relief. Instead of stressing about one bad race, I took responsibility about the change in training and we turned our attention to the Great American Cross Country Festival and a very good Loudoun Valley team. We went on to win Great American with a record setting performance, which set up another bigtime showdown the following week with Newbury Park at Clovis.

Make adjustments. Knowing that they beat us handily the first go round, we needed to run smarter. We know Woodward Park, home of the Clovis Invitational and the California State Cross Country Meet well, and we formulated a race plan to beat them this time. The first thing we did was play out **their** race plan. What would they do, when would they do it? How should we run to beat a team using those race tactics? Knowing they had two of the fastest guys in the race, and that they were a very confident team, we assumed they would all go out hard. This presented the opportunity we needed. If their 4-7 went out too hard and died, which often happens on this course, then we could put our pack in between their guys and win. While the teams were being announced, I let my boys know not to focus on their team, but on how to run the course correctly, to commit to the race plan and let the chips fall where they may. At the first mile Newbury Park did exactly what we had expected, plowing the front and owning that position, compiling only 40 points. We had been patient and laid back the first mile, scoring 208 points at that point in the race. Our boys knew that they didn't need to chase Nico Young or Jace Aschbrenner, we just needed to move our pack in between those guys and the rest of their athletes to win. Slowly but surely, we moved up that 2nd mile, erasing an almost insurmountable lead making it Newbury Park 65, Great Oak 97. Our guys were pushing, eating up packs of guys in front of them, while the younger guys from Newbury were starting to fade due to a hard early pace. Chris Verdugo and Cole Sawires Yager pushed into the top 10 at the finish, with 8th and 9th place finishes. We ended up putting six guys in front of their #4, to seal the win 57-65! Trust your race plan, make adjustments throughout the season, and have your team prepared to compete, no matter what the early results are.

Recharge. Take time away, recharge your mental batteries, identify your team's motivation to move forward again. After

Woodbridge, we spent time identifying and renewing what our seasonal goals were. We knew what we wanted to do, and we focused on training and executing when it mattered. If a team beats you in the season, they are doing you a favor. They are showing you what your weaknesses are. They are showing you what you need to do to beat them when it matters. Never take a loss as final. We ended up losing to Newbury Park by 4 points at Nike Cross Nationals, but we learned we can compete for the national title every year and will continue to build a program that focuses on doing just that.

PART II: BUILDING AN ELITE TEAM

When you set out to build an elite cross country team, you are putting together so many pieces that you have to understand that it isn't a short term timeline, this is a many year venture. You have to go all in! To build an elite team you have to have an idea of what you want to build, and that vision has to drive you. It has to be the little voice in the back of your head that allows you to pull 12-14 hour days, every single day. It has to be a vision that is so strong that things like watching the NBA or the NFL stop being important. You start to cut out the things that don't matter to your vision, and you start adding in more time to build.

What is an ELITE Team, in cross country anyway? How do we define what an elite high school cross country program looks like? I've always defined "elite" teams as teams that are consistently at the top, they are always in contention for championships, no matter what time of the year it is. Granted, all teams have ups and downs, but elite teams are still really good on their off years. *The names of the athletes change, but the results stay the same.* Elite teams or programs are often run by elite coaches. These coaches have gone out of their way to try to incorporate every training component, every mental aspect, every cultural concept they can to improve their teams on a consistent basis. These teams don't disappear, because someone is at the helm making sure that they are always heading in the right direction. Joe Newton from York High School in Illinois, Dan Green from The Woodlands High School in Texas, or Pat

Tyson from Mead High School in Washington are all examples of high school coaches that <u>consistently</u> produced elite teams. To get to that level, you have to be good or even great at almost all aspects of the coaching spectrum. These legends built teams that year after year were some of the best in the country. In this section we will be looking at where you are at now, and what it takes for YOU to build a championship level elite team on a consistent basis.

CHAPTER FIVE: OUTWORKING YOUR PEERS

There is no doubt that winning requires time, effort, and dedication. What I have found in my years of talking with coaches is that a lot of them truly don't understand how many of those things it really requires. To be a great coach it is going to take countless hours, and most likely a lot more hours than many people want to put in. How would you rate yourself as a head coach? Where would you like to be? Without question, the only real way to move up the coaching ranks is to put in the work, and to be great you must consistently outwork your peers.

When I was a first year coach, the only thing I really had was the fact that I was hypercompetitive. You may have better athletes, more athletes, better prepared and experienced athletes, **but I want to win**. For me to be able to do that, I must convince as many athletes as I can to join my sport, buy into my training, and I must create an environment that keeps them out there with me year over year. Over time I learned how to build a training plan for each season I coached, and eventually one that made sense for the entire year. I developed the ability to communicate well with assistants, parents, and the athletes on my team. I learned how develop a rhythm to my coaching that gave my athletes the best chance that they had to compete with elite teams. Over time I learned how to listen. That doesn't come naturally to someone who is hypercompetitive. It is learned out of necessity. To become a winner, you have to learn to listen to the most important people in your world, your athletes.

What does it mean to outwork your peers? It means reading more books and adopting the things you learn. It is making lists of questions you have and finding the answers. It means more fundraising and interacting with people who can support your program. Outworking your peers is making your sport the place students on your campus want to be, because you are always putting in the time to do the next thing that will make your program more appealing. I put in a fridge and had my parents provide chocolate milk, protein drinks, Gatorade, water, and set up an area for protein bars. We have branded our team through a Nike sponsorship and created amazing gear for them to wear. There is no limit to the ideas you can come up with that take your time and energy, but if you want to be successful, come up with more than everyone around you. Make your team the place to be on your campus!

Making Cross Country THE Sport on Your Campus

Let's face it, football is king. At least that is what we have always been told. I personally played football and love the sport, but there is no reason that a cross country coach has to believe that any sport on their campus is more important than their sport is. We are the rulers of our own kingdoms, and if we don't allow other sports to outshine us then we are the ones who control the narrative. We are the ones that project to all those around us that we are the best, and that we have no plan to play second fiddle. The most intense dude on our campus isn't a football coach, he is the cross country coach. Fear no one.

What is the image of cross country on your campus? A bunch of goofy kids that don't care about the results, they just like to hang out and run a little bit? If you want to be the IT sport on campus, you have to mold an image of cross country that it is THE place for the elite athletes on your campus to sign up. That image includes winning, style, effort, intensity, and a relentless approach at practice. Athlete's want to know that their personal time is not wasted. Practices should be legit, and everyone on campus should know it. The tough guys aren't on the football team, they are the beasts on the cross country team who fear nothing. Everyone wants to be part of a winner. Build one and make sure everyone sees it.

Highlight your elite successes and your athletes as they accomplish impressive things. If everyone gets an award just for showing up, then you are establishing your culture as a place that just breathing is a win. It should be a meritocracy, where those that do get the prize. That draws athletes that know if they put in the work, they get the credit. Nobody had to pass them a ball, there is no defense to ruin their race, they don't have to sit the bench, they get a lot of control of their results. Elite athletes like that and will be drawn to it if you make it the place to be. Use the daily announcements at school, social media, your classroom if you teach, and any other avenue you have available to show off your program. Show them as hard working, fearless, winners, and as intense competitors. Nobody wants to go hang out with a bunch of geeks, but they will go hang out with athletes that have a killer mentality.

Build a brand. Make your athletes the best outfitted team on the campus. Our athletes are draped in the latest and greatest Nike gear, and everyone else on the campus notices it. I have students all the time ask me if they can get a jacket, or some shoes, or a t-shirt. I always tell them you have to be on the team to be cool enough to wear that gear. Our stuff is so wanted, other sports on the campus purchase our left overs for their athletes. When students on our campus see a cross country athlete, they see someone who is fearless, has the best gear, has been taught to be respectful and hardworking in the classroom, and someone who sets the standard for expectations on our campus. This intimidates some, but draws many others who want to be a part of something special. How is your team perceived on campus? What can you immediately change in your program that ups the visibility of your program on your campus?

Phases of Growth as a Head Coach

As a cross country coach, you will go through many different phases of growth on your way to being elite. Not everyone takes the same path, and some coaches skip some paths based on their experiences as a runner or other areas of expertise they bring with them into the coaching arena. Most coaches will go through the phases, as many of us won't learn what it takes for certain situations until those situations are upon us. Where do you sit on this scale and what phase do you plan to get to?

The Soles Phases of Coaching

Introductory Level Coaching usually is the place where a coach starts, where they have some background in running or athletics or teaching. Typically, they have a lot to learn when it comes to building a training plan, building their numbers on their team, and putting together all of the phases of training to have their team ready to compete at the end of the season. Introductory coaches typically have smaller teams, shorter practices, do what their coaches did with them in the past, and aren't 100% sure why they are doing most things. Often, they just coach the kids that come out for the team and don't do a whole lot to get anyone out for the team. They are missing many training components and have a lot of holes to fill in their coaching abilities. To move on from this phase, a coach needs to attend coaching clinics, find a mentor, read a lot, and use trial and error to find things that work in their program.

Follow the Leader Level Coaching starts to see the coach looking outside of their program for guides on how to improve their team. The go to clinics and take back what they learn and often copy things straight across to see how it works in their program. Their training plan has pieces from lots of different coaches they have read about or listened to, but they don't always know how those pieces work or if they will help their kids improve long term. They start finding ways to build their roster and up the numbers on the team. Their training plan is a patchwork of what they believe works and what they have seen work for others. These coaches start to reach out to their coaching peers to ask questions as to what they do and why they do it. They are starting to understand the why behind some of the concepts they are applying. To move on from this phase, a coach needs to start setting goals and begin attempting to win meets.

Advanced Level Coaching begins when the coach starts focusing on building a team that can compete for victories at local meets and invitationals. This level starts to see the coach reaching out to top level coaches around them looking for ways to improve and get their team to the state meet, and a more competitive position in the state picture. Their training plan is adjusted yearly, things that didn't work are taken out, new things they have learned are added in. They have become successful at getting out a good group of 9th graders each season, and keeping them in the program long term. They are now applying race plans and tactics with their teams that work and make sense. The athletes on the team understand that their coach knows what they are talking about, and they believe in their coach. To move on from this phase, a coach needs to start consistently winning league titles, qualifying to sectionals, and competing for state meet qualifying spots on a yearly basis.

State Level Coaching sees coaches who have developed significant experience, can build season long or yearlong training concepts with a specific outcome in mind (usually the state cross country meet). These coaches understand when to push and when to hold back, and develop a rhythm to their seasons. They are very good at roster management and athlete development, often drawing many new athletes to their team each season. They expect to make the state meet each year, and are working on ways to be in contention each season. They sit down with their athletes and plan the season in advance, and give their athletes a voice and stake in the success of the program. Everyone they interact with knows they are a great coach who knows their stuff. These coaches expect their athletes to focus solely on cross country, and to buy in 100% to the team goals and expectations. To move on from this phase, a coach needs to consistently contend for and win state championships.

Elite Level Coaching is where we start to see coaches who have a developed yearlong training plan, and a very specific end goal in mind (usually state or national meets). Elite coaches typically have won multiple state titles and have made it to nationals consistently. These coaches have figured out the nuances not only in training, but in working with people! Their parents and athletes have bought into their program and understand the goals and expectations and are a part of the success that the program is having. Everyone understands their roles! The parents know what they need to do to keep their child healthy and improving. The athletes understand the expectations and what it takes to improve, usually being a big part of the goal setting for the team's season goals. The assistant coaches are empowered and able to execute their role without fear of their head coach, but rather in synch with the goals of the team. These are the coaches you hear about on the Internet regularly, and the ones that understand that getting to and staying at this level requires talented athletes and always developing athletes to keep their varsity roster at a competitive national level. These coaches spend a lot of time developing athletes and focus on all of the athletes on the team, not just the varsity. Elite coaches spend 3-6 hours a day outside of practice building and improving their team! To move on from this phase, a coach needs to consistently win state championships, and consistently contend for national championships.

Ultra-Elite Level Coaching has maybe five to ten coaches across the country at this level of competition at any point in time. They have everything down to consistently be one of the top teams in the country. These coaches are the ones that are always in the conversation to win the national championship, and somehow season after season seem to reload back to an elite level, despite losses to graduation. These coaches can control decisions made by other teams' parents, athletes, and coaches, as well as the media just by making a comment or tweet. Ultra-Elite coaches do everything elite coaches do, but they do all of it just a little bit better. These are the coaches that set the standard and are the example for the rest of the coaches in the country. To get and stay at this level, you must sacrifice everything and stay passionate enough to stay on top.

Where do you fall on the above scale? Where do you want to get to? Only you can decide how much time, effort, and dedication you will put in to get to the next level. If you want to be Ultra-Elite, then everything else in your life will take a back seat to building the best program you possibly can. Most people don't want to sacrifice like that, especially long term. Being an elite coach is not a seasonal or periodic thing. It is a full time lifestyle choice. Before we won our first state championship in 2010, the first thing I thought about when I woke up in the morning was "what can I do today to help us win a state championship." When I got in bed at night, I would ask myself "what I did that day to help us win a state championship." It was everything, and it happened because it was everything.

Growing Your Numbers

Have you ever seen a team show up with three, four, or even five school buses full of kids for a cross country meet? Intimidating, isn't it? Building a large and competitive team can take time, but the benefits are many. Obviously, the more athletes you have training at a high level, the better your chance of finding athletes that adapt to the training and excel. These athletes will continue to feed your varsity machine for years! It is critical that you spend as much time as you can growing your numbers each season so that you can always have a team ready to take on the best.

The first thing you need to do once it is legal for you to do it, is to email every incoming athlete coming into your school for the following year. Work with the ladies in the front office, get a spreadsheet with all of the emails, addresses, and phone numbers of the incoming 9th graders and build a recruiting spreadsheet based on what you know about the athletes coming in. Email every incoming frosh an invitation to the team. Send out individualized emails to the athletes you have identified as critical to the team's future. Give them information on the team and a way to sign up like a Google Form, and encourage them to do so. Track who is signed up and who you still need. Call the ones that you haven't heard from. Be relentless. Do a home visit and bring athletes from your team, videos, and anything else you think will help get them out. You must get an answer from the key incoming athletes! That isn't always easy, but it is definitely worth it.

Many years ago, I emailed Haley Dorris' mom 20+ times when she was an incoming frosh going back and forth about her trying out our team. Haley was a very good Irish Dancer, and we knew that her older sister was a great athlete. I did everything I could to get her to give it a try. Once she finally relented and came out to try it, she was an instant fit with the team and she slowly built her way into one of the best runners in California. Had I given up at the first couple of times I was told no, we would have missed out on one of the best athlete's we ever coached. Her senior year she ended up 7th at State in cross country, and later in the spring she was the Master's Champion in the 1600 in 4:44! If you know someone is key to the team's future success, do everything you can to get them to join!

Many coaches that have coached for years will tell you one of the easiest ways to build a team is to mine families. Get out sisters, brothers, cousins, family friends, and anyone else they know! Every athlete you bring on your team is a potential recruiter for future athletes on that team. Family members tend to share the fun they are having being a part of your program, which in turn will draw in other members of that family. Twins and triplets are often really amazing to have because they push each other harder than the average person is pushed. Many times, one twin wants to run and the other one who is just as good will pick a different sport so they travel different paths. Isn't that sweet? No, it isn't! You need the other twin too! Make sure that you find a way to get them to switch. Invite them, be super nice to them, tell them you will make them a superstar, do whatever you have to do, but get them on your team. Why? Almost every twin that didn't start out in our program that I have been able to get to join us later on down the road, has played a huge role on our team. Don't assume the first assessment they make as an 8th grader is the correct fit for them long term. Do a little persuading and find a way to have them help your team.

A great tradition we have done over the years to encourage athletes to think about our team, is to deliver a little letter with a t-shirt once they graduate from middle school. Obviously, this is different depending on your state rules, but for me it has always been once they graduate, we can try to get them on our team. Assign this task to returning leaders, so that they can take ownership of the athletes that come out and the building of the future of the team. I usually identify 20-25 athletes per gender and get them some old shirts and a letter to deliver with a message from the kids that we want them to join. *You will never hurt someone's feelings by telling them they are wanted.* Identify who you need from the incoming 9th grade class, and send your minions to butter them up. If it adds even one good frosh to your team that wouldn't have done it originally, it was more than worth your time!

Usually, it takes a decent size team to get to the elite level consistently. Smaller teams can hit that level for a short run, but eventually run out of talent. One of your main objectives each summer is to identify, recruit, and win over the best incoming runners to your school. It never hurts to fish some old ponds as well. Remember all the 9th graders that told you no last year? Keep a list of all of them and reach out to them again and see if you can get one that changed course at some point in their high school journey. Never stop fishing, you never know which athlete will change your results and the direction of your program.

Frosh Recruiting Scale:

1-Star - Very beginning runner, limited talent, may have limited interest. Often parents are trying to find something for their child to be involved in, or the athlete wants to use XC on their college resume. Limited growth or potential long term.

2-Star - Usually a beginning level runner, some basic talent, may have limited interest or join to spend time with friends. May stick it out for a couple years. Some will pan out, some will become depth, and every once in a while, you will get one that works extremely hard and makes the top varsity group.

3-Star – Often, these are the athletes that we build our programs around. They can run but don't show tremendous immediate skill. Over time, if they work hard and build up their skills, they can move to the varsity group and contribute. Most high schools have lots of these athletes, but you usually have to compete with other sports for their full commitment. If you get 10 of these on your team in a class, 2-4 of them will usually turn into varsity contributors over time.

4-Star – Very skilled runners with a lot of upside. Often good athletes that know they have a lot of talent. Each class has a few of these athletes, but many coaches are vying for their attention on campus. These are the kids you have to win over if you want to compete for state and NXN titles! Your goal is to identify these athletes in middle school and speak to them as soon as it is legal in your state. Winning often comes down to how many 4-star athletes you can consistently recruit of the frosh coming into your school.

5-Star - Potentially a state champion level athlete, with a female athlete as early as their first year. Typically, extremely talented and motivated towards the sport. Usually play another sport such as soccer that you will need to slowly extract them from over time. Parents likely to be very involved, which can be a good thing if they buy in. Overall, it is hard to fail with a couple of these on your team at the same time. Usually these athletes are few and far between. If you have a chance at one, do everything in your power to get them on your roster.

Utilizing Social Media

For many old timers out there, the thought of social media is one that makes their insides turn. The truth is though, as a coach you must go where your athletes are! If the athletes you need are on social media, you need to find a way to go out and get them using that medium. If you are not going to learn it and utilize it, then you assign it to an assistant coach that knows it, a parent that can do it, or you hire a student at the school to manage it for you. It is critical to get the information for your team out there immediately so that athletes, parents, college coaches, and fans outside of the area have a chance to find out what is going on.

Twitter is a great chance to share news and build up your teams' profile. This gets your info out to media outlets, college coaches, and fans so that they can stay up to date with where your team is at and what they are up to. This is a great place to post images, short videos, team links, fundraising opportunities, and more for your team. It is also a great way to follow and connect with other teams and media outlets. Twitter is the best way to quickly share "news" for your team to many people. This is a promotion platform, promote your team with it.

Instagram is where a lot of the athletes are currently, which of course will change over the course of time and new social media platforms are released. Instagram has a picture posting function that allows you to share images, videos, and information for the team. It also has a story function that you can use to get info out to many in a fun way. I often use stories to get out announcements to my athletes that I need them all to see quickly, as they are usually on this platform.

Facebook is typically used by alums, parents, aunts, uncles, older siblings, grandparents, and friends of the family that don't live in the area. This platform has a large base of users, mostly college age and up. Many have been on it for years and will "friend" the team page so they can keep up on results, fundraisers, and more. Use this to build up a following for your booster group, and for them to share information to parents for fundraising and events.

Snapchat, Reddit, YouTube, and other social media platforms are other ways to reach your fans. If you do not currently have a social media presence, ask yourself what some of the benefits might be? College exposure for your top athletes? Important info being shared to runners who will be matriculating to your school in a few years? The opportunity to wow parents and athletes with how great your team is? Ultimately, you have to decide what benefits and negatives there are for using social media, but in my opinion, there are a lot more upsides than down.

One of the recent trends that has popped up on many teams is athletes doing vlogs. These little YouTube sessions that they compile can really share your teams' culture and fun with many other people. I have had a few vloggers on my teams and it really helps me when it is time to recruit the incoming 9th grade class, because I can send them a vlog video of a trip we went on and show them what an amazing group we have and how much fun it is to be on our team. Find your vloggers and guide them for what you are looking for!

In today's environment, having a strong social media presence is critical for an elite team. Plan to utilize at least 2 of these and be prepared to have someone consistently updating them so that they do their job of reaching athletes. What you will find over time is that you can develop a large following of people, including future runners!

The Plan – 10 Steps to Winning the Big One!

There simply isn't a better feeling than the moment you realize your team has won the big one! For each of us the "big one" is different, but the feeling is the same. Winning the big one might be winning a league, section, or state title. If you are one of the very lucky few, you might even win a national championship! To pull this off you need have an elite understanding of the plan and the steps that it takes to win when it matters.

10 Step Plan

1. Sit with your athletes and get them to believe that **winning the big one is their goal**. Nothing else on this will matter if they don't believe they are the ones wanting this. Your one real job is to set this in motion. Like Michael Jordan said in the Last Dance documentary "It all started with one little match."

2. Take a look at the **key training components** section of this book. Find the components you are missing in your program and implement them. Remember, your goal is to create aerobic athletes, not distance runners. The high school race is simply too short to focus on pure aerobic over athletic ability. What are you missing from the list? Add it.

3. If it is possible, **travel to the course** during the regular season every year to compete and get a feel for every nook and cranny. That course has to feel normal for you to have your best days, and your athletes have to be able to see it in their minds to plan for it.

4. Once a week or more at the end of practice, take your athletes through a **visualization of the race**. Always have them finding a way to win for it, even if athletes fall, get hurt, run well, run horribly, etc. Have them see it in their minds so when they are on the course, they are so ready that they no longer think about

execution, they just react to what they already know and are programmed with.

5. **Up your mileage**. The best teams in the nation are running 60-80 miles a week. You won't beat them running 30-40. Your training plan has to have your athletes not only fit enough to compete with the best teams, but also so fit that they can make it through all of the rounds of the post season. If you want to win the big one, you better have a plan for your mileage and it better be in range of the teams you have to beat.

6. You are missing 2 athletes from your team that you will need to win this meet. Who has them? If you are building a boys' team, they aren't going to be 9th graders, so someone on your campus has them. Probably soccer or basketball. Find a way to get them on your team. Home visits, emails, athletes on your team recruiting them, sell them on the ability to compete on a national level, etc. Find a way. The elite teams have amazing front runners, but they win with depth! You want to win the big one? *Fix the holes on your roster!*

7. **Build a cross country season schedule that gears everything towards the race you ultimately want to win** (example: resting some top athletes at your league finals meet to have them fresh when you need them). This is roster management at its finest. Rotating different pieces around to have the key athletes ready for the race that ultimately matters. Add meets to your schedule that give your athletes a chance to take on the best teams. Run sweepstakes races and don't hide from anyone. You won't win the big one by underpreparing your athlete's competition wise! Compete!

8. **Develop a race plan for the course and the teams you will face** that works for your line-up, and will have your team ready to run their best race on race day. Obviously, every race is different and no set plan will be perfect, but many courses have nuances that are important to know and master before attempting to win on them. Watch videos of teams who have qualified to the championships and break down film. What was the winning team's strategy? What did the 2nd place team do?

Who went out fast and how did they finish? Who started slower and moved up? Make sure your athletes have a detailed step-by-step plan on how to own the course on race day, and that they are confident about implementing it. Know your competition, and what their potential race plan will be so you can execute against it.

9. **Show up to the race with them mentally and physically prepared**. No nerves, all business. Fear happens when you are in the realm of the unknown. It isn't scary to take a test you already know all the answers to, and your athletes won't be afraid to compete when they know they are prepared at the highest level possible. Program them to win.

10. **Win**! Execute the plan on race day, knowing that you did everything you could for your team to be ready to compete for that title. There are very few things in life better than watching a group of athletes set a goal, put everything they have into chasing that goal, and then watching it come to fruition! Take time to soak it in and enjoy the moment with your kids.

Mastering the plan above will help you hone your team into a championship winning machine, one that steps to the line with confidence and without fear. Remember that it is a process that you are trying to master. As the years go by and you master each step, your teams will get better and better and closer to locking up that coveted championship!

As you begin to outwork your peers, you will see your teams slowly but surely starting to pass up teams you used to lose to. Coaches that coach 2 hours a day aren't going to beat coaches that put in 6 or 7 or 10. How much time are you willing to put in? Who do you want to beat? Who are you willing to learn from? Most the coaches that I have seen on the right track that didn't make it to the elite coaching level simply gave up too early. Great Oak opened in 2004. We won our first state championship in 2010. It took us 12 seasons, until 2015, before we were able to develop to a level as coaches to be able to win an NXN Championship. If you want to be great, be willing to outwork everyone, and be willing to do it for many years. Decide where you want to go, and go after it! It doesn't happen overnight!

CHAPTER SIX: WHERE ARE WE GOING?

I've always been a road map guy. Let's map out our journey and include the stops along the way so we can better see what challenges we may face throughout the season. How can you try to get somewhere if you don't even know where you are trying to go? How do your athletes show up every single day and give you everything they've got if they don't know where the promised land is? If you know where you want to get, then you can empower leaders to get you there. You can draw up a plan attack to conquer the challenges along the way. Most of all, you can foresee the effort it will take and prepare the sacrifices everyone will need to make accordingly.

Set goals that are challenging enough to drive you through the season, but not so unrealistic that nobody really believes in them. Really sit down with your athletes and find the items that create a fire in everyone's belly. The best goals we ever set as a team were the ones that everyone showed up talking about each day. Everyone knew why we were there, and everyone put in the work to accomplish those goals.

Pick amazing leaders. Surround yourself with great people, but also surround yourself with people that have your program's best interests at heart. Bring on coaches that bring something special to your team. Select captains that complement each other, work hard, and care about the outcome. Do not make captain picking a popularity contest, make it a selection process that selects leaders that will keep everyone accountable to the goals that have been chosen by the team.

Create a theme or motivational concept for that season. To be honest, I don't always do this. Why? Sometimes the team concepts stay the same from season to season, but eventually enough athletes and personalities change that you need to go in a different direction. Sometimes you get wronged and it provides such motivation that you just have to mention it to fire up your team. As a coach, go into your season with a motivational plan, and be ready to use things that you find along the way to power through the season.

What is Our Motivation?

When building your road map for the season, make sure to plan out when and where the motivation is likely to occur. We are facing this team here, we have to travel a long way to there, and did you guys hear what this team said about us? These little bits of motivation that you can preprogram on your road map give you a giant heads up to what is coming your way as the season progresses, and can make you look like a prophet for seeing things coming before anyone else does.

One of the things I have always tried to have on our road map is the next little thing the athletes are working towards. You can't just say "oh we are here, time to win state" because too much happens from the start of the season until you line up against the best. What you need to do is have little carrots along the way, little pitstops on the road map. I've used things like qualifying to our team camp in our time trial, earning a varsity uniform, proving yourself to be worthy of running in a sweepstakes race, or getting selected to make our travel trip to name a few examples. These short term motivational pieces help the athletes to enjoy and work their way through the season without stressing one big goal the entire way. This gives us the chance to have fun, while still being on course to win the state title.

Who do we have to beat? When we opened in 2004,

89

Murrieta Valley was the best combined cross country program in the state, finishing well on both sides each year. Steve Chavez had that team running like a well-oiled machine, and no matter how good other teams got, they were always in the running for the title. They also happened to be in our league, so for us it was easy, right out of the gate. How do we beat Murrieta Valley? The obvious answer was we needed to get bigger as a school (we started in 2004 with 9th and 10th grades only), we needed to find more talent, we needed to develop that talent, and we needed to _not fear them_. As we developed and closed the gap with Murrieta Valley, we needed to go into attack mode, and give our athletes reasons why we could beat them, not reasons why we couldn't. The best way to develop confidence in a distance runner is to show them how fit they are. When they know a 3 mile race or 5k isn't far for their fitness level, they won't fear the race. When they are fearless in a race, they can attack it! We eventually took down Murrieta and began looking for new foes. For our girls' team, who was ahead of our boys' team at this point, it was Dana Hills in 2007 and then moving on to Saugus in 2008. We didn't hide from anyone, we searched out the meets they would be at, and the races they would be in so that we could measure ourselves, test their strategies and strengths and weaknesses. Each time out we closed the gap and found a way to chip away at their advantages. This doesn't happen overnight, but if you can build a team that likes to hunt the best teams in your state, you will eventually start taking down the best.

Who do you need to beat and where can you face them? What goals or pit stops are you currently missing on your road map to have your team ready to beat the best at the end of the season? What evolution does your team need to make for your to be the best team in your state? Design a road map, fill in your missing pieces, project your outcome. Did you win it all? Why or why not? Who are you missing to get you over the top? Is it an athlete? An assistant to help you? More money for trips and bigger meets? Identify your team road map, and sit down with your coaching staff, your athletes, and even your parents to find a way to make that road map happen!

Top 16 Meetings

Early in my career at Great Oak we qualified for the CIF meet and were competing for a chance at a state meet birth which was difficult to do in Division 1 for such a young school. A few of the girls had pretty good races but most of them didn't do that well, and after the meet some of the girls told me that most of the girls didn't really want to move on or were scared to qualify. One of the girls stated, "I don't even care if we make state, I'm ready to be done." Hearing this was very hard and frustrating! Why would a team that I had spent all this time building and honing for CIF not even care once they got there? It was in that moment I realized that I wanted it a lot more than my athletes did. Something needed to change!

The season had ended and I spent lots of time thinking about why we ended our last race like that. Ultimately what I realized was that the athletes were only going to work so hard for my goals, but that they would work much harder for theirs. They didn't have a buy in at the level that I did and saw themselves running to accomplish my goals instead of something that they were passionate about. We were stuck in a spot where they loved the team, the experience, the fun, but had no real buy in for the hard part, the championship season. I had to find a way to get the athletes to want to win at the same level that I did, and get them to set and buy into those goals so that they would give everything to accomplish them. Ultimately, I settled upon a meeting format that would allow them to set the goals, set parts of the schedule, and give the athletes a very big voice in how the season would go.

Now every May we get together as a top 16 varsity group to plan out the next cross country season. This meeting typically consists of the varsity coaches and the top 16 selected returning athletes and everyone has an equal voice at the meeting. The hope is that we come out of the meeting reflecting on how we did the previous season. What did we do well, what needed to change, and what steps could we take as a team to make those changes? What were the key changes to the schedule that the athletes wanted? The athletes really love that part and always spend a lot of time debating which national level meet we should travel to that season. Most of all they enjoyed that they were the ones setting the goals!

Why Athletes Set the Goals

A strange thing happened after I implemented these meetings. The athletes started working harder. They would say "Coach, if we are going to win state, I have to be faster!" They began to care about what they ate, injury prevention, getting enough sleep, and finishing all of their miles. No longer was I forcing them to perform for me, I was now their guide on how to realize the goals they wanted to accomplish! Your job is to not only become their guide, but to make sure that they see you as their guide. A guiding light in a sea of darkness, the one person who can lead them to the promised land. You will stop having to discipline, and start having to explain how they can get better, because **they** want to improve!

Another great thing that happens when the athlete's set the goals, is that parent complaints now have to deal with the fact that you aren't pushing them to your goals, you are pushing them to their child's goals. You aren't dictating to them, you are guiding them to what they have set out to accomplish, and parents have to acknowledge that. Parents have to see that you are the coach, you set the rules, you keep everyone accountable, but you keep them accountable to what THEY said they wanted to accomplish. Your athletes get up every single morning and work for the team goals, not for the coach's goals. When everyone in your program understands that, roles and dynamics change for the better.

One big thing I have found with this, is that no matter

how bad your team wants it, they probably won't stay motivated 100% on their own. You are still responsible for keeping them focused on their goals. Sometimes as a coach, you have to be the gas in their engines. You have to keep the fire lit. If they veer too far off the path, you relight that fire underneath them! Be their guide, not their taskmaster.

Short Term vs. Long Term Goals

A big misconception that I see often is that athletes have a good grasp on goal setting. They don't! It is our job as coaches to help guide them through the process. What are the short term goals that your team needs to set throughout the season to guide them along their path? What are the long term goals? Let's break down the differences and why they are important.

A short term goal in cross country can be something as simple as running a time, getting a place, making a specific team, or qualifying to camp or a specific meet. These goals are often the little things that move us from point A to point B on our road map, and on down the line. These goals should be attainable in the near future, usually are a bit easier to attain, and should help athletes set new short term goals to accomplish after they accomplish one. Many years ago, in our program, we only gave out the Red GO uniforms to our varsity athletes in our program that had earned them. Everyone else got the basic uniform or the old blue varsity uniforms we had. At the beginning of the season, many of our athletes set the short term goal to prove their worth for a varsity uniform. It was a big deal when athletes got it for the first time, often celebrating with their family that night. These small accomplishments teach your athletes how to achieve the little things along the way and give them a small boost of motivation to go after the next goal. Your job as a coach is to give them lots of opportunities for little accomplishments or short term goals along your road map that your team has set up. What have you set up in your program to help your athletes set short term goals?

Long term goals are usually a lot harder to attain, and are set somewhere further out in the future of the road map. Maybe it is making varsity as a senior, or getting to go on the travel trip in a future year. Long term goals are ones you are always working towards and tend to be the end goals of the road map like winning a state title or maybe even winning NXN.

One of the biggest mistakes I see coaches and athletes make is setting a goal to qualify for a certain meet, like the state meet. The problem is once you arrive at state, there is nothing left for you to accomplish, you have already hit the goal! Many times, this is why you see a lot of the teams at state or NXN happy just to be there, not worrying about the race or the results because they have already arrived at their destination on their road map. Nothing more to see here, we are done is the happy look on their face. Instead of setting a goal to make it to state, set a goal to finish top 5 or top 10 at state or on the podium. Give a realistic goal that keeps your team motivated upon arrival at the meet. Although making it to a big meet is exciting, you as the head coach are missing an opportunity to prepare them for that event because they have already checked out upon hitting the goal. Set long term goals that are difficult, keep your entire team engaged, and something that is worth accomplishing. Nothing is better than celebrating something three or four years in the making!

I have always tried to explain my frustration for a poor performance to young people in a way they will understand. Winning a specific meet like state is my video game, but I only get one try per team per year. I have to wait 365 days to try again. A painful loss can haunt you, and you won't get to see if the adjustments you make even work for a year. Like Christmas, it only comes around once annually, so make sure to use that entire year to fix everything that didn't go right, or to expand upon the things that did! A great way to do that is to write down all of the good things, bad things, and fixes you see the night of the meet while it is fresh. I often do this on the notepad on my phone and email it to myself to put in a Word file somewhere for later use. It is harder to remember the nuances of the meet, the personnel, and what was said months later after the wounds have started to heal. Take note, work on finding fixes, and improve for the following season.

Individual vs. Team Goals

I've always felt that an amazing team produces great individual performances. We have had our share of elite athletes come through, and none of them lost out on the experience of high school cross country by us focusing on the team before the individual. I believe an athlete learning how to sacrifice their individual identity for the good of the team teaches them just about every life lesson they will need once they enter society. How to listen, share, care, sacrifice, lead, follow, and how to be a good teammate. All of those items are critical in the workforce and in relationships as an adult.

Our program has been blessed with some amazing athletes over the years in cross country. Destiny Collins and Tori Gaitan won individual state titles in xc, both leading their teams to state championships by just a few points. They delivered as individuals, but were doing so because they knew how important their role was in helping the team be successful. They were happier to see their team win then to win the individual title themselves. Destiny's state title came her senior year, after an awful race at the sectional meet. She ran so poor that coaches accused me of playing with their heads when she won state. The truth is, even the best athletes can have an off day. Her teammates rallied around her at the sectional meet, and she rallied for them at the state meet. It is that belief in each other, that bond that is shared that gives athletes the strength to move on in the face of adversity. Tori was extremely prepared to run at the state meet her junior year, and was very good at taking instruction and applying it to her race. She listened and applied what she needed race plan wise, ran smart, and utilized her speed over the last 400m to secure the win. Both of these young ladies had set the goal to be the state champion and watching them cross the line in 1st was something special to be a part of as a coach.

Individual Goals are very powerful, and can be the fuel in the tank of your athletes to try to accomplish amazing things. You need to have a conversation with each of your athletes about what their individual goals are, why they set them, and any additions or advice you have for them. Find out their why. What is it that motivates them to be great? For some it is making a certain team, or getting the varsity uniform, or getting to run sweepstakes or state. For others it is all about time and championships. Learn what fuel they are putting in their tanks, and add to it as needed throughout the season.

Our athletes set our team goals. This is our guide as a coach to decide what the team's focus will be. When setting team goals, focus on 3-5 main things they want the varsity group to accomplish (you can set other goals for other levels). Spend the time going into the season looking at what the main goal is, what some road map markers along the way would be, and really what the athletes are willing to go all in for. Usually the main goal will be some sort of success, and your job is to guide them and keep them realistic. If you have never won a league title and your athletes want to win NXN, you may need to focus on one step at a time. Build your team goals each season, progressing to more difficult challenges each year. This forces you to get better as a coach, and for them to work harder as athletes to get there.

Managing Elite Talents Versus the Average Joe

My college coach used to call them "Mercedes Athletes" because if you got a good one, they would make you enough money to someday buy a Mercedes. Elite athletes are hard to come by, and often you have to work to keep them with you because they are good at more than one sport. Many of the best cross country runners start out in youth soccer and are eventually stolen away by an ambitious cross country coach. Truthfully, elite athletes are all around us, but we are looking for a specific kind in cross country. We are looking for one that can win against the best!

The question I get from a lot of coaches when they get an elite athlete is "what do I do now?" Elite athletes can be scary, because everyone recognizes that they are very good and spectators want to see how they develop over time. Often elite athletes have many fans, even some on the opposing teams. Destiny Collins was so popular in high school that she was busy signing autographs at many of the dual meets she was at for the team, when she wasn't even racing. Tori Gaitan added a few thousand followers after the Arcadia Invitational on social media her sophomore year. So, once you get to the point where you realize that you have a truly special athlete on your hands, you need to have a plan in place for their training, their college recruiting, working with their parents, and the media.

Training an elite athlete can be a little bit different from working with the average athlete on your team. Elites may require more work, more specific training, more of your personal time, but at the end of the day what they really require is your focus. Athletes that are on the long term development plan don't need the varsity head coaches time in the moment, there are other coaches for that. Elite athletes need you to watch their every move. They need to you to make sure that they aren't overdoing anything, or underdoing it. That they are relaxing when they are supposed to be relaxed, and intense when they should be intense. Are they eating enough? The right foods? Are they handling the mileage? Are they limping? Coaching an elite athlete means that you live the ups and downs with them. You don't take risks with them, you protect them from you, from their parents, and from themselves. To train an elite athlete, you have to make adjustments to their training plan. How good are they? Can they compete for a state title this year? Should I push a little harder here or there so they will be ready, or hold them back? What is their biggest weakness? I always try to figure out how I would beat my athlete if I was coaching their chief competitors. What strategy could I employ that would take down Destiny Collins? When I can think like my competitors, I can prepare for their every move. If they want to make it come down to a kick, I'll make sure my elite drops them before we ever get there. If they don't have a kick, my athlete will be sharpening their kick like it was an axe. Don't pigeon hole your elite athlete into the same training as everyone else. Many things will be the same, but figure out what you need to do for them to fix their weaknesses and have them prepared for their time to shine. The best thing any coach can ever do when training an elite athlete, is keep them healthy and developing. When in doubt, rest.

College Recruiting is a very important part of working with your elites. Remember that you are there to help, you are not there to become their manager. Don't talk scholarships with college coaches, let the parents do that. Your job is to help map out the pros and cons of each university they are looking at. What is a fit and why? What isn't? Let them know that college coaches move around a lot and that the one recruiting them, may not be there in a couple years. Help them pick a school that fits their wants for academics, weather, location, scholarship money, team fit, and how big of a role they want to play. Some kids want to be a big fish in a small pond, and others want to be the slowest on their new team so that they have to work their way back to the top. Help them map it out, and let them make the decision.

The first thing that I like to do with my elites as we get to their Junior year is sit down and discuss what they are thinking. Where would you go if you could go anywhere and why? What type of weather are you looking for? What type of weather would you hate to run in? What degree do you want to get? What is more important, winning or a full ride scholarship? Are there any specific things you have to have (beach, elevation, certain part of the country, etc.)? Once we have a pretty good answer to these questions, we can narrow down schools that fit what they are looking for. Once they start to form a list, I have them email the coaches and begin a dialog. Remember that many of the top colleges don't want to recruit, they want the athlete to show that they are interested and then they will put in the effort. Seems counterintuitive, but that tends to be how it works. Don't wait for colleges to come find your kids, have your athletes searching out their perfect fit. Start a dialog with them when they are young, but really start to nail down the details by their junior year.

Once they leave for college, you have to let them go, you can't try to keep the option of whispering in their ear. Let them go, let them grow, tell them to buy into their new coach and new training, and whenever they come home, give them lots of love! There is a transition from coach to fan that must occur, and it is important to give them space as they move on. For most of us, we get our athletes on a 4 year contract. Know when that contract is up, and when to transition to their biggest fan.

Working with their parents can be an amazing teamwork, or a total nightmare. I've been blessed with the majority of parents I've worked with that had elite athletes really understanding the importance of supporting their athlete's coach. Those parents want to see their athlete succeed and are willing to step back and let you do your thing. Some parents have to interfere, it is in their nature. When a parent won't allow me to coach their athlete, regardless of how good that athlete is,

I let them know they are welcome to leave and find a better fit for their family. To be successful in coaching elites and working with their families, you need to be honest, communicate the plan for their athlete, listen to what they are hoping to see, and show them why certain things have to play out in specific ways. Many parents do not understand what is going on for cross country and I've found if you let them know what the plan is and how you plan to get their child to the next level, they tend to want to be team players with you.

The Media can be your best friend, and your worst nightmare. As a head coach, I highly recommend that you control your media. What that means is, you let them know what is acceptable and what is not in working with your program. If they treat you right, they can have amazing access to your elite kids and the program. If they don't, then they get nothing. If you are a coach that works with an elite team or athletes on a regular basis, make sure that you have a friendly understanding with your local and state level media. If they break that trust, don't work with them. No interviews, no coverage, nothing. They need you more than you need them, they need content. Make sure they understand that to get that content from you, that you set the rules. That may include how they get contact with any elite athletes' you coach. The reason for that is you don't want the media to get in your athlete's head. You want to shelter them from that situation. Spend time with your elite athletes explaining that when they get good, the detractors come out...even for high school kids.

Building a trusting relationship with your elite athlete. Your job as the coach of an elite athlete is not to become their popularity manager, it is to protect them from what the limelight brings. The media, the college coaches and their texts, emails, and phone calls, and especially the social media comments. I always tell the kids to let me be the bad guy, and for them to focus on getting better. Take that pressure off of them and let them know you are in their corner. I believe that if you want to build a great relationship with an elite athlete, you have to trust them and they have to trust you. It takes time to build that. When they see your plan is working, they will trust you more. When they see you care about their health and safety, they will trust you more. When you give them a little extra leeway to test themselves in big races, they will trust you more. Build a championship relationship with your athletes, and have their back whenever you go out to war with them. You are their shield, be there for them.

Keeping the JV working to become varsity elites. Some of our all-time best athletes started out as average frosh that slowly developed over time. Many don't make the top 7 on the boy's side until they are seniors. With these athletes, I remind them of all of the hard work they have put in along the way and why it is important not to waste the opportunities they have created for themselves. You never know which 5' 4" frosh boy will be 6' 3" and ripped as a senior! Develop all of them and find the diamonds!

CHAPTER SEVEN: TRAINING FOR SUCCESS

Building an army is one thing, but training them is another. You can have hundreds of athletes on your team and still not win Nike Cross Nationals. At some point you are going to have to create a training plan that prepares your athletes for success on the course. The beauty of training is that there a million paths to Rome, you just have to find the one that works for you!

What is your philosophy for training distance athletes? Who have you read and who are you planning to read? Vigil? Daniels? Jay Johnson? Dr. Jeff Messer? We all build a training philosophy from somewhere, even if we don't realize it. There isn't a lot of new in the training world, most is recycled workouts from years past. Why? Because those workouts have worked. The ones that don't eventually get discarded and stop being passed on. I've seen programs that basically are designed around doing tempos every day to ones that were just pure aerobic monster builders, running 100 mile weeks. The key to being a great coach is figuring out which workout components you want to use, where and when you want to use them, and then being smart enough to evolve and try new things each season to develop the perfect fit. Take out what doesn't work, and try new components. To be successful, you need to be ever evolving as a coach.

The Great Oak training concept was born from Dr. Joe Vigil, and evolved to add in a little bit of everyone I read, have heard speak, or concepts I wanted to try like High Intensity Interval Training. We have tried everything under the sun, and eventually settled on a consistency style that focuses on daily doubles. No specific workout is life or death, but all workouts combined build fit and talented athletic distance runners. Our goal is for every athlete on the team to be the best version of themselves that they can be, regardless of talent. Athletes like Cameron Hylton, Aric Reza, and Shannon Emery started out as good but not great runners in our program. Their desire and work ethic to be on the line when it mattered, made them some of the best in the state their senior years. We don't define our success as coaches by just the top 7, we define it by how many athlete's we can build. How good is your "B" team? That is a question we are always asking ourselves.

Summer Cross Country – How to Build a Championship Base

Talk to a lot of cross country coaches about their favorite time of year, and most of them will tell you it is the summertime. Why? Because we get an opportunity to focus almost 100% of our attention on the athletes, and they get to focus a lot of their time on getting better. Many of the improvements we see in our athletes happen over a long summer break, where they are upping their mileage, focusing on bonding with their teammates, and setting big goals for a new year. Summer is refreshing. It is like someone hands us a clean slate as a coach or athlete and it is up to us to decide what we want to do with it. Like many of you, I want to use my summer to get to know my freshmen, shore up any holes in the program from the previous year, and usually to try something new. Utilize your summers to get the most bang for your buck over the season. This is base building time, go big!

Mammoth Cross Country Camp is a special time for our program. Our athletes qualify to attend camp via our time trial on the first day of summer practice. Typically, the top 16 on each side get the honor of going with us. This keeps athletes focused throughout the summer, because they know that day one, they will be tested for something they value. When you give your athletes work to do on their own, ask yourself what motivation they have to actually do it? How will you hold them accountable? Camp is the perfect thing for us because everyone wants to go, and why wouldn't they? Mountains, lakes, trails, pro runners all over, and amazing runs and hikes abound.

Obviously, nobody builds a gigantic elevation base in a week at camp. The point is to provide a getaway together, a team bonding trip where athletes can get to know each other better, and can learn some of the key things they need to master for that season to compete with the best in the country. Our typical itinerary is a morning workout, some free time, a clinic where they learn something, lunch, a team activity or trip, afternoon workout, and some team bonding to end the night. By the end of camp our team goals are solidified, our leaders are identified, our team is bonded and ready to work for what they want to accomplish, and the coaches have a good feel for what the season will look like. I highly recommend doing a summer camp with your kids. Even if it is just for a couple days, it is worth it!

Your athletes will come back excited, and they will share that excitement with everyone else!

Summer is the perfect time to start doubling. It is one of the best ways to build mileage, and it increases your athlete's ability to burn calories throughout the day. Not only should your team be trying to build a solid base for the season, but you should take the success of the summer and build on it over the course of the next few months. If they are running 50 miles a week over the summer and things are going well, maintain or build from that throughout the season. Use the summer as a springboard to mileage consistency. Any athletes that come in out of shape should be in a beginner group, building their mileage back up. Don't make the mistake of putting a talented athlete in the varsity group, if they don't have the mileage base to back it up. They will just get hurt and they won't help the team long run. Build them up and add them to varsity when their bodies are ready to handle that workload. Make them earn that opportunity.

The best way to have a great summer is to have a training plan for all your key groups. Everyone knows what they need to do, and what the expectation is coming in to the start of practice. Have something that is a check or reward for who worked hard and who didn't. Establish that summer is the base of your season. November might be the state meet, but June, July, and August are when you prepare your team to win when it matters. Build a big base, team bond, build your athlete's strength and athleticism, incorporate the frosh, and form a team identity.

20 Key Endurance Athlete Building Components

As you build your training calendar each season, there are some key training components that are important to master to ensure that your athletes will be ready at the end of the season. Obviously, some of these are more important than others, but to get to the elite level of coaching, you should have the majority of these somewhere in your training plan. Look at these components as the ingredients to a soup recipe. Most coaches will use many of the components below, but how you use them will differ from every other coach in the country. Will your soup taste better than theirs? Here is the breakdown of the components we do in our program:

- **Practice Communication** – Let's face it, most of us start practices with a meeting of some sort and that is good. Outline the important things your athletes need to know about for the week, the day, and for the practice. Fundraising, upcoming meets and events, and anything else you feel is pertinent for your athletes at the time. This is also a great opportunity to give a thought of the day, or to have one of your assistants share a thought. I tend to share my news and plans for practice and ask if any of the assistants have anything to add, any of the captains, and then any questions anyone has before having them start their warm-up.

- **Warmup/Cooldown/Stretching** – Everyone is going to see their warmup and everything in between to their cooldown differently, and that is ok. I highly recommend that you get away from the old school jog for 10 minutes and stretch. The truth is you need to be developing athletes, which means you need to spend a lot of time doing a dynamic warmup that not only gets them ready for their workout, but also one that works on the fundamentals of speed, strength, and form. Cooldowns don't have to be anything fancy, but should be a way for athletes to shake out after a harder effort. They aren't always needed. Stretching is something you can create a routine for, or just leave to the athletes to do on their own before they leave or at home depending on how much time you have available for it. It should be at the end of practice, not at the beginning.

- **Speed Ladders** – Our goal is to create endurance athletes, so speed ladders help us to create more coordinated, agile, and faster paced individuals. We spend about 20 minutes in the middle of our warmup on speed ladders each day, completing about 10 different exercises. Think about how uncoordinated a 9th grader is when they come into your program. Speed ladders are a great way to turn them from a rookie who can't walk and chew gum at the same time, to a full-fledged speed demon. Be consistent and focus on accuracy, speed, and consistency.

- **Core Routines** – At some point in your daily practice schedule, there should be some sort of core routine or two. Core routines not only help your athletes build strength, stability, and injury prevention, they up the athleticism that you should be working hard to create in your athletes each day. Create and perfect core routines and have your captains or a coach lead them each day. Make this a priority and it will pay off for you!

- **Strength Routines** – We have also added in strength routines that we do that help add strength for our athletes in specific areas. Utilizing the sand, we do a lower leg routine that helps prevent shin splints and builds stability in the legs. We do routines with 5 pound weights to help strengthen our shoulders and arms for hills and fast races. Think about the areas you want to focus on creating strength and build programs athletes can do at practice, or at home for extra credit.

- **Mileage** – The most important thing about mileage in your program, is that both you and your athletes believe that it is the exact right amount for them to stay healthy, and for them to get faster over time. Obviously, mileage may be different for every athlete on your team, but the overall design of where their mileage is will most likely travel very similar paths. Think of mileage like stairs with steps. Frosh might be on step one, sophs on steps two or three, JV on steps four or five, varsity on steps six or seven, and your elites could be on step ten. The rhythms and patterns to their workouts are often the same, but their mileage is different because they are on a different step. So, in our varsity group, our frosh might have a 3 mile run, our sophs might have a 5 mile run, our regular varsity might have 7 miles, and our elite athletes might have 9 miles. They can all run together, and they often do, but different athletes will be dropped off earlier than others because they are on different steps on the stairs of our mileage program. Find the sweet spot for your program mileage wise, and always be consistent in challenging it!

- **Hills** – Your best way to build easy strength is to get on the hills. Not all areas have a lot of them. Sometimes it is a ramp coming out of a parking lot or a street, sometimes it is a driveway, and if you are lucky it may be a grass or dirt hill. We do a lot of 10x60m hill sprints, where the athletes sprint to the top and walk back down (we don't run down due to the stress it puts on the body which can up an athlete's chance of injury).

Sometimes we mix it up with moderate paces up and down continually for a specific amount of reps or time. Another great way to utilize hills is to have a 600-1000m loop that has a big hill in it so that they have to practice Vo2 Max style hills. No matter what, you should have hills in your training once a week for a lot of the season.

- **Stadium Routines** – The Great Oak Stadium Routine takes 30 minutes and consists of 3 parts. First, we do 10 minutes of **every step as fast as the athlete can go**, with a walk back down. Second, we have the athletes do **perfect form lunges** to the top of the stairs, focusing on arms and posture for 10 minutes. This works on strength and form. Lastly, we do 10 minutes of **every other step, race to the top** (versus a teammate), with a walk back down. This focuses on explosive speed and competition development. Whatever you decide to do for your stadium routine, remember that some of it needs to focus on explosive movement.

- **Vo2 Training** – Early season Vo2 work is often Fartleks in our program. As the season progresses, we switch over to more 5x1000, 8x800 type work with anywhere from 90 seconds to 5 minutes in rest between our reps. Developing this in your athletes, is raising their ability to handle intensity during exercise. The stronger they are here, the better they can handle the pressures of racing. This should be a component about once a week in your training calendar, depending on how you create cycles. Build their heart's ability to process oxygen, and they will be ready to race!

- **Lactate Threshold Work (Tempos)** – Tempos are a very common training technique. We often refer to this as lactate threshold work as it takes many different forms. Most of us do 3-6 mile tempo runs, where athletes are running 80-84% of their 5k race pace for the duration. We often tell our athletes that they are running at a pace that they could talk, but they probably wouldn't want to. It is great to mix these up! We do 3x2 mile tempos, 5,5,5's where they run the first five minutes at 70% effort, the second at 80% effort, and the third at 85+% effort without stopping. We usually take 3-5 minutes in between and do 2-3 sets of these. It is a great LT workout to see who is race ready. One of my favorite tempo workouts is to run a fast 800, give the athletes 60 seconds, and then send them out for a 2 mile tempo. This does a great job of preparing them for a fast race start where they will eventually settle in. We do 2 sets of these and they are tough, but great for race prep. We usually do 1 set of lactate threshold work a week on average.

- **Running & Core HIITs (High Intensity Interval Training)** – This is a component that most are not currently doing, but they should. Aerobic running doesn't burn off all of the fat you want to burn on your athletes. To do that, you must have other types of training to accomplish a significant EPOC (excess post-exercise oxygen consumption) burn. HIITS are amazing at targeting the areas that running doesn't, and helps your athletes develop strength, athletic endurance, and get as fit as possible without adding very much mileage to your program. The beauty is it doesn't take a lot of time and is easy to add in. You can find a lot of HIIT programs ready for use on the Internet or YouTube. Try some out or use the ones I have in the index of this book. It will make your athletes better and more fit!

- **Plyometric Routines** – Plyo routines are critical in strength development, explosive power, athletic ability development, and helping athletes stay healthy. A beginning level program should incorporate at least box jumps and box or stadium step ups. A more advanced program should have 2-3 routines or a 5 station rotation that athletes move through in an allotted time. Carve out time once or twice a week to really build your athlete's abilities through plyometric training.

- **Med Ball Routines** – There are many different exercises that your athletes can do with a med ball that will help develop strength and explosiveness. We usually do these twice a week with our plyos, and have an A and a B routine. Make sure you purchase enough for at least your varsity group to work with, and have time set aside in your practice schedule for them to be able to consistently get them done. Some of my favorites are explosive throws up and down, squats with a med ball twist, and lunges with a med ball twist. What kind of ways can you use a med ball to increase your athlete's athletic ability?

- **Visualization** – Use this mental training component to practice a specific course or race that you must succeed at consistently. Our program focuses a lot on Woodward Park, because that is where our state meet is held. We spend 10-15 minutes once a week programing our athletes with the experience, emotions, and expectations of how to be successful on that course. Make sure to set aside time to use visualization to prepare your athletes for their toughest challenges.

- **Iron Intake and Monitoring** – There is almost nothing worse than ending up with athletic induced anemia as an athlete, which in layman's terms means you have low Ferritin. Ferritin is the iron stores in your body, and you need those stores to help transport the oxygen molecules you are bringing to the muscles in your body. As a coach you need to make sure your athletes are getting tested at least 3 times a year, and that you are helping them manage their iron intake, either through diet or through supplements. In our program we shoot for a Ferritin score between 80-100, which allows our athletes to perform at their best and not have any anemia side effects. Everyone is different, so work with a doctor in your area to master this for your program.

- **Diet** – I am not a dietician, but I have brought in a few for our program over the years. The basics are; eat healthy, eat enough calories, get rid of the bad foods, and replace them with healthier and whole foods. High school kids want to eat all kinds of junk. As a head coach, you need to guide them on what to take out of their diet and what they should be putting in. If you are weak in this area, hire a nutritionist to develop a plan for your team. I've even had amazing parents that have developed meal plans for the team and taught the kids and parents how to prepare them. Make it simple, set the rules (no soda, no energy drinks, cut out the white sugars, cut out the wasted calories like Starbucks) and eat good quality whole foods.

- **Sleep** – This is probably one of the harder components for this generation. From teachers piling on homework in AP and IB classes, to a myriad of technological distractions, our athletes are getting less sleep than they used to. You have to teach sleep to the athletes and parents so that they understand that this is when you heal from all of the hard work you are putting in. There is no supplement, magic pill, or recovery workout that can keep you healthy and improving more than sleep can. Encourage your athletes to get 8-10 hours of sleep a night.

- **Competition in Practice** – One of the most important things you need to do in practice is teach your athletes to compete. You don't want them to try to figure out competition in races, you want to bring them to the line as a veteran of competing and learning to be a champion. Winners win. It is your job to find your winners and have them on the line when it matters. There are times to hold your athletes back, and times to let them rip it up. Often little things like the HIITS, certain parts of a core routine, or a stadium routine race are great chances for them to learn how to challenge themselves to be their best.

- **Injury Prevention** – The best injury prevention is communication. Make sure your athletes feel comfortable sharing with you any aches and pains they have. I find that younger athletes don't identify the difference between soreness, having a minor area that is hurting, or being injured well. Build a report with your athletes and let them know the warning signs for critical injuries, as well as what they will probably need to run through. We can't take 2-4 weeks off every time an athlete gets shin splints. What we need to do is make modifications to soft surfaces, focus a lot of strength training on their lower legs, and modify the mileage and workload as tolerable. Buying stationary bikes, ElliptiGO's, or other cross training equipment can help. Having injury prevention strength routines or band routines can be great for injury prevention. I find that putting in a lot of time on core and strength has helped our program stay healthy, even though they work hard to compete for state and national titles each season.

- **Nike Cross Nationals Soft Surface Training** – One of the things that has helped our program tremendously as we prep for competing for national titles, is doing soft surface work. There is hardly any soft surface in our area except for sand, so sand is what we do. Remember when doing this type of training, you have to tie everything they are doing physically to the mental components they will need to be prepared for at nationals. You are preparing them to run in soft surfaces physically, but also how to persevere through the discomfort of something that feels very foreign to many of them. If your goal is to run at NXN, prep them every couple of weeks with a specific soft surface workout.

A program that includes all of these components at a high level will see their athletes improving at a higher rate than the programs around them, and eventually see themselves competing with the best in the state. Which components do you have already in your program? Which ones do you need to expand upon? Which components do you have that you don't find on the list? Why do you think that is? It is up to you as the head coach to evaluate every component in your program and eliminate what isn't making a big impact, replacing it with something that can help your program improve.

How to Maximize Practice Time

Many coaches across the country fail to understand the importance of using the time that they are given with their athletes wisely. Every component you decide to use should have a purpose, and you should know what your athletes are getting out of it. You should be adding in components that are working, while taking out ones that don't seem to be enhancing the overall ability of your athletes. I see things in other programs all the time that I would like to do as a coach, but if I don't have time in our training schedule, or I'd have to take something else out to make it work, I have to be able to justify that the new component better prepares athletes than the one I'm taking out. Most of us get two to three hours a day with our athletes. What will you do to maximize that time each day?

Why is using all the time important? I've personally had coaches brag to me about getting practices done in an hour or less. Great, what components did you get done? What components could you have utilized the rest of that practice for? When setting up a practice, your ultimate goal is to make sure that you are utilizing the time you have to properly prepare your athletes for the mental and physical rigors of racing. Yes, you can semi prepare an athlete to run cross country by putting them through an hour or less of practice a day, but you will not be developing athletes. The athletes with a lot of talent will do well simply because they are great runners naturally, and the ones with less talent won't have much effect on the varsity season. You aren't really coaching; you are more or less a talent manager. Whomever is the most talented makes varsity, everyone else is JV or Frosh/Soph. To create an elite team, you have to have a plan that makes your talented athletes' elite, your pretty talented athletes developing towards elite, and your average athletes raising the standard of "average" to a place that your average athletes are better than a lot of team's varsity athletes. Talent will always be a huge deciding factor, but if you can get 2-3 really talented athletes, and you can build 2-3 elite varsity level athletes over time, then you can develop an elite team. Why would you skip components that in the long run will create you the missing pieces you need to win? You have somewhere else to be other than the top of the podium?

Filling in with components you are currently skipping will lengthen your practice time, but also help you fill in the gaps in your training. Everyone is doing a lot of the same things, so what separates your team from everyone else's? Mileage? Talent? Size? Workouts? Uniqueness? Ultimately, you have to put together your training plan to focus on creating a recipe that develops athletes, keeps them healthy, strengthens them physically and mentally, and prepares them for the rigors of the toughest races they will face in a season. There are many paths to Rome, and you have to build your path with the components that will work in your school, your weather, and your culture.

When designing your practices, what is your focus? Is it on getting in specific workouts? Just running? How do you outline a consistent practice schedule so that your team is regularly preparing to be the best it can be? Which practice outline below makes the most sense for your program and the improvement of your athletes?

Basic practices should include these components each day at a <u>minimum</u>:

- Team Meeting
- Warm-up
- Strength or Core Routines
- Main Workout

- Cool Down

Elite practices may look more like this:

- Team Meeting
- Warm-up with Speed Ladders and a Running HIIT
- Strength/Core Routines
- Main Workout
- Cool Down
- Core HIIT or Plyos or Additional Strength Routines
- Visualizations
- Stretching Routine (with program or on your own)

Mileage Concepts: What It Takes to Compete Against the Best Teams in America

The easiest way to improve your team from one season to another is to raise the mileage your team runs. Making just that change will give you better results for the season in most cases. Cross Country is a sport literally built around the concept of running miles in the hopes you will be more fit than the person next to you on race day. The real questions are; what should you be asking your athletes to do? What mileage totals make sense for your population, weather, location, and training style? How do I get my athletes to buy into working hard enough to be successful? How much is too much or too little? Only you can answer these questions based on your situation, but to compete at the elite level as a team you need to be capable of winning major invitationals, and to do that you need to have a team that is fit enough to compete with the best teams in the country.

Anyone who attends Nike Cross Nationals regularly and has the chance to discuss training with many of the best coaches in the country, can tell you that most of the best boys' teams are consistently over 60 miles a week and many of the top girls' teams are over 50 miles a week. The top athletes at Great Oak average 65+ a week throughout the cross country season. To compete with the elite teams in the nation you need to have a talented team, and they need to be running 50-70 miles a week on average to be able to last until the beginning of December to compete at NXN.

If you decide to build your teams up to those levels, realize that it takes time. You might up them by 7-10 miles more per week in cross country, then up them a little more in track, and then another bump up the following cross country season. Don't just tack on 20+ extra miles a week so you can be elite. Remember, the fastest way to injure your athletes is to skip steps. Slowly but surely build your team up mileage wise over time and give them a chance to adapt to the new workloads as you are building. This adaptation should be mental and physical. Mentally, your athletes need to know and believe they can handle the extra workload. As they discover that they can, their confidence will go up and they will be ready for more.

What should you be asking your athletes to do to build more mileage? Depending on where you are at right now, it may be as simple as adding a few more miles to each of your workouts. If you feel like your afternoons are already maxed out, look to add some morning runs to help add some mileage over time. 1 morning run of 4 miles adds 4 miles. 2 morning runs adds 8 miles, and 3 would add 12 miles using that concept. How long is your long run? Can you push your athletes to add another 2-4 miles there? Find areas in your schedule where your athletes can get in some double days and extend out what you can over time and you will see your weekly mileage totals start to get to where you want them to go.

Getting buy in from your top athletes is key. Make sure to discuss with them the changes you are making and why you are making them. As they get stronger and more fit, they will buy in. As the top athletes go, the rest of the team follows. If your top athletes are running 60 miles a week and doing really well, everyone else will want to emulate what they see from the top guys. Don't just tell them to shut up and run. Instead, project with them the improvements the increased mileage will bring to their performance, and help them with icing, sleep schedules, and recovery so that they can stay healthy and ready to compete when the time comes.

How much is too much? That is up to you to decide as a coach, but it is usually the point where injuries and fatigue outpace the perceived aerobic gains you believe your team is making. So, if you decided to build them up to 80 miles a week. Some would adapt to it, some would struggle with it, and some would get injured. At that point, does running that mileage give you an advantage or actually set your team back? What happens to the math if you did 70 instead of 80? Does the math switch in your favor? Are more athletes adapting and staying healthy? What about 60? 50? You as the head coach have to find your sweet spot as a team. What works well for you to aerobically grow you team's engine without losing many athletes to injury or fatigue or burn out?

The truth is there that there is no correct number. Whether you run 30 miles a week or 80 miles a week, neither is right or wrong. People will always have opinions on what you should be doing, including parents, athletes, assistants, and maybe even administration. At the end of the day it is your decision to make, and you need to build a training plan to puts your team in position to be healthy, fit, and ready to compete when it matters. If you want to compete at Nike Cross Nationals, if that is your top goal, then you will be challenging your teams to build up over 50-60 miles a week consistently long term.

The Importance of Core & Strength in a Complete Program

Every single day, we put in 30-60 minutes of core work in our program. We don't do this as a filler, we want our athletes to be as strong and injury resistant as possible. Typically, we consider core anything from right under the chest to the tops of the knees. Keeping our athletes strong in this area increases strength, muscle endurance, explosive power, injury resistance, and stability. Your kids can only run so much, but you can spend a lot of time strengthening their bodies. Find the components that work for your group, your location, and your goals.

We have been blessed to have Coach Noble as our core guru since the start of our program in 2004. He has worked tirelessly to make our athletes stronger and more injury resistant. Having someone take ownership of this component has tremendously helped me as a head coach. Find someone to help build a championship core program with your team.

One of the biggest mistakes many coaches make is to do core at the end of practice. The reason that is often a mistake is that athletes are all coming in from their runs at different times, and many athletes try to find reasons to leave after their run (dental appointment, doctor appointment, homework, mom is there to pick them up, have to go to their job, etc.). We schedule core in a dedicated time slot right after our warm-up to make sure that we get it done, otherwise you will find many of your athletes missing out on a lot of the core and the benefits that go with it. Make it a priority and formulate a plan for when in your daily schedule you will have it each day.

In our program, we do 7 different core routines throughout the week. We also do Core HIITs (High Intensity Interval Training), Plyos, Med Balls, Box Jumps, and many other types of strength building components. Think about your athlete's total physical athletic ability. What can you do as a coach to increase EACH area of their athleticism through different strength training components? Where are your athletes weak physically or athletically? What do you need to add in to fix that going forward? There have been several times in our program where a bunch of athletes got the same injury around the same time. This is a critical piece of data that shows you that something you are doing is putting stress in a certain area, or that your core and strength development is lacking in developing strength in that area. Identify your athlete's weaknesses and look for solutions.

Supervision is critical for success. Assign these components to an assistant to run to make sure the athletes are meeting expectations. Captains can do a great job as well, but it depends on the captains. Have a plan in place for what they are going to do, when they are going to do it, and make sure they learn the routines. A great team can run through the expected practice without a coach ever saying a word. Now that isn't the best way to run a practice on a consistent basis, but if you just started practice by spinning your fingers in the area to symbolize to get going on the warm-up, would your kids be able to finish it if you left? If you weren't there could they and would they do everything they knew they were supposed to do that day? If they knew why they were doing it they would. Teach them what they need to do to be great, and allow them the ability to show you they want it, especially the leaders. Give them a chance to lead. Once they have it, pull your assistants out and let the athlete's run those components. Watch, adjust, motivate if needed, but allow them to grow as a team and as leaders.

It is my opinion that some sort of core strength activity should be taking place in a program each day if you want to maximize your athlete's long term development.

High Intensity Interval Training (HIIT)

Many years ago, I began looking for something that was missing in our program, and I couldn't quite figure out what it was. Something that tied together the training we were doing with the athleticism and fitness I wanted from our athletes. I discovered High Intensity Interval Training through the gym, and have found that utilizing this type of component with my teams has increased many areas in their abilities that have helped improve them as cross country and track & field athletes.

Running HIITs have become a year round staple in our program. They have lots of benefits, including increased stamina, strength and form improvements, teaching how to make race moves and how to respond to them, and calorie burning. In our program, we tend to start with about 10 seconds of 96%+ effort, then we blow the whistle and the athletes switch to 20 seconds of 50% effort for recovery. We build up duration over the course of the season and they end up about 3 minutes and 30 seconds worth of ups and downs. We do run HIITs right after our warm-up is completed, usually 3-5 times a week. They are a quick and amazing way to improve your athlete's ability to respond to moves made in races! They are a daily reminder why we do what we do. We do everything to get faster.

Core HIITs we do three times a week, with a goal of added strength and fat burning. This component is finishing off a training session with a specific calorie burn. We usually have multiple routines that we rotate through, and we do 1-3 sets. We may start at 20 seconds on and then 15 seconds recovery march at the beginning of the season, building up to 45+ seconds on and 10 seconds recovery. Even basic components like fast push-ups, crunches, or burpees can create a good boost to heart rate and help your athletes with an afterburn effect called EPOC or Excess Post-exercise Oxygen Consumption. That little extra burn of calories (100-200) and strength gained doesn't do a whole lot each day, but over the course of a season or a year or a career? You can see the effects on the athletes on our team. They are more fit than the majority of the competitors they face.

HIITs are a pretty quick and easy way to up your athlete's fitness and racing ability. They help your athletes become better athletes. If they only gave each of your athletes a 2-3% boost to their overall ability, wouldn't that be worth the time? How many kids does 3% move them up at state? You want to win championships? Look for every advantage you can find and give it a try. HIITs might be just the component you have been looking for.

Visualizations: Programing Your Athletes for Race Day

In 2011, our girls team finished 7th at state. We had prepared the girls physically for the race, but mentally they were not ready. To be honest, they were scared to death. This was eye opening for me, as our 2010 girls were able to win the state title against one of the most loaded fields I have ever witnessed in California. What I learned was they were ready physically, but not mentally for the rigors of the post season and specifically the state meet. I needed to adjust everything to prepare our teams to be ready for the 2012 season. And adjust I did.

The first thing I did was focus on visualizations, which we needed to do to practice a course that was 6 hours away. I upped the competitiveness and expectations of all athletes at practice. Our 1st period workouts became longer and more difficult, and our mileage was raised. All told, I made over 20 different adjustments to the program after that state meet. It was so intense that Haley Dorris asked me why I was punishing our girls' team for losing. I had to explain to her that I wasn't punishing them, that I was trying to help them never have to go through a post season like 2011 again. By the time the 2012 season rolled around and our girls had adjusted to the changes, we went on to not only win state that year, but they ran over a minute faster per girl from the year prior, and you could have doubled our score and we still would have won. Never be afraid to make adjustments when you don't feel like you are preparing your teams as well as you believe you can. Sometimes you have to scrap everything and start over. From 2012-2018, our girls won seven straight state titles because of those adjustments.

Adversity and loss can be the best thing that can happen to your program. Don't hesitate to utilize it.

What results did we see from adding in visualizations in 2012? The amazing thing was that not only did 2012 go well, but our boy's teams started to see success as well. All of our varsity athletes started to see and believe that we could win state championships. Our boys' team went on to win their first state title in 2014, and state and NXN titles in 2015. A lot of the reason for this success was that our athletes were not only physically prepared at a high level, but they were so mentally prepared that the California State Meet stopped being scary, and started being an expected stop to claim our yearly prize. The athletes believed they were 100% ready for the state meet race when they lined up.

The best way to ensure you do visualizations is to put them in your training plan. Pick a day for a specific visualization you plan to do each week. We focus on the state meet every Monday after our hill workouts in our program. Everyone knows that we will be doing a visualization that day, and comes out of them just a little bit more prepared for the course and event that the state meet is. You can use these for more than one meet or one course, but to really see dramatic results, figure out where they are needed the most and focus on that race.

What do our visualizations look like? Coach Noble takes one varsity gender, and I take the other. We have them lay back, close their eyes, and relax as they listen to the sounds of our voice. We don't haphazardly take them through the state sequence, it is planned. It is a programming of their minds so that when their racing, they don't have to think, they just responded to the things they see around them. They are mentally prepared for the different types of races that may occur. They are prepared for what their race should look like and many execute flawlessly. Getting different coaches preparing them also helps fill in gaps one coach might have. Mix it up, try new things, have fun with it, but utilize this opportunity to prepare your team.

Example Coach Soles Visualization of Woodward Park in California:

You find yourself riding the bus on the way to the race. You are nervous, but calm. You look around and your teammates seem calm as well, and that gives you confidence. Today is the day you have trained for, waited all this time for. Today is the day you earn your ring, and you want that more than anything. As the bus arrives at Woodward Park, you remember the words of your coach echoing in your ears "It's just another race." You find strength in this, as you always race well. As you walk over to the team area with the other athletes racing that day, you gain assurance from the looks you get from the other teams as you pass. They know what is about to happen, they know what you are about to do. You get to the team area and make sure everything is ready. Your racing flats are where you need them, your bib is on, you have eaten what you need to eat. It is time to start warming up. Your heart races, but you tell yourself that is more excitement than anything. You are excited! Excited to finally show everyone what you can do at the great Woodward Park. Starting the warm up together, you can feel the strength your team has. These 7 girls together are on a mission, and you know you will give each one of them everything you've got! You realize it isn't about you, it is about the team goals, about making every step about the girls next to you. You are ready. As the warm-up finishes, coach tells you there is 5 minutes until you need to be standing in front of him. You take a deep breath and go through your routine; one you have done countless times. You get on your racing shoes, take a sip of water, and head over to coach. The look in coach's eye is different today, more intense. You can feel the passion he has for you today, and that gives you strength! "Today's the day ladies. Today we complete this journey together. No matter what happens out there, the coaches will care just as much for you after the race as we do before it. Do your best, rely on your training, and have fun." You head out to the starting line together, marching single file like an army on a mission. You get in your pre-race strides and realize that you feel fresher than normal. The little tweaks the coaches have made to training have left you ready, feeling fast and determined. Get out, relax and control your race you think to yourself. A deep breath and you are ready. The gun sounds and you are off! It feels like a dead sprint, your heart is racing, but you tell yourself to relax and get position, you are excited that you got out well. Slowly but surely relax and get the position you are supposed to be at when you get to Coach Soles. As you go by him, he yells at you that you did it right, you put yourself in the right position for a great race, now follow the race plan the rest of the way. **It goes like this for the remainder of the race...**

Ultimately, your goal is to **program** each part of the race (What they see, how they process it, what they do, and how they feel about that action). Have them ready for all scenarios, all parts of the course. Train them how to start, how to move, when to move, where to move to. This is your chance as a coach to truly control the outcome of a race without ever stepping foot in it.

There are many benefits of visualizations. Confidence, reaction time, preparedness, and most of all, programming. I tie everything they do and see to an emotion. I program how they will react to many different scenarios, so if one of them occurs, they just respond and keep going. No panic, no fear, no overreaction. Just do what is supposed to happen in that scenario and move on. The last thing you want your athletes doing when they get into a race is thinking. You want them responding to stimuli with responses they are programmed with. Have your team programmed and ready long before they ever hit the key race in your season and you will see a dramatic increase in their ability in your target race.

10 Elite Concepts Every Coach Should Know

Elite coaches understand that to be the best, you should be doing or seeing these ten items on your team:

1. If it isn't helping you win, don't waste your time on it.

2. Be ever evolving as a team and as a coach.

3. Often elite teams are as much about ego management as they are training to win.

4. Your team is only as good as the athletes on your team! There is no coach alive that can win without talented athletes. Great athletes can make average coaches look amazing! If you want to be competitive, you will search out and bring elite athletes into your program on a consistent basis from your feeder schools.

5. To consistently compete at an elite level as a team, you need to travel nationally and compete against the best teams in the country.

6. If you can't teach or coach a needed component for your program's success, find someone who can.

7. Know when to be nice, when to be intense, and when to be cutthroat.

8. Have a killer instinct, and teach a killer instinct to your athletes. The national championship meet is loaded with *hunters*, not *gatherers*.

9. All coaches will make mistakes. Your job is to make fewer mistakes than your peers on a consistent basis.

10. When you start winning, nobody likes you as much as they pretend to.

CHAPTER EIGHT: NETWORKING AND RELATIONSHIPS – THE POWER OF COMMUNICATION

Coaches don't spring forth from the ground like corn. They are instead built over time through hard work, dedication, time, and most of all their ability to absorb and receive information. Almost all championship coaches started at the bottom and worked their way to the top. Some moved up faster than others, but everyone starts at a first practice with a first group of athletes. We usually make a ton of mistakes and work to find answers to fix those mistakes. What most of us find out along the way is that it is a whole lot easier if we make friends.

I've made countless contacts with other coaches along the path from beginning coach to successful status. Some make a lasting impact, and others come and go, but almost all of the coaches we interact with teach us something. Knowing that, it is important for every coach out there to go out of their way to build a network of coaches that they can rely upon as the years go by. This network will be there to help you when you have questions. It will be there to support you when you lose the big race, or to congratulate you when you win. As you build your network, you will find the benefits of doing the same for other coaches as well. Don't be an island, be an innovative communicator. Someone who reaches out to others to help them, for them to help you, and to hopefully make each other better!

One summer afternoon I had a meeting scheduled where I schedule all my meetings when coaches want to talk to me, my favorite pizza place. Now this coach wasn't a distance coach, he was a sprints coach at a rival school. He didn't want to talk about anaerobic training or training in general. He wanted to ask me how I became successful. He wanted to add me to his coaching network. He wanted to have someone that had seen almost everything there is to see as a high school track coach as someone he could reach out to in case he had questions. He wanted to get better. I ate my pizza, answered his questions, and to this day I still learn from him. His sole desire was to improve his coaching network, because he knew it would make him better. That is the goal. Challenge yourself to get better each day!

Tapping Resources: Avenues to Get Better

We are fortunate today that help with our many coaching questions is right around the corner. We are all one Zoom meeting away from another group of coaches to ask questions of, to try to hone and improve as coaches. Many coaches don't ask questions because they fear that they will look inept. I got to where I am today by asking many of the best coaches I could find, some of the dumbest questions they have probably ever been asked. I didn't care if my questions seemed dumb or simple to them, I cared about finding out the answer. You have to seek knowledge at a level that sets your ego aside, and frees you to go to a clinic or a Zoom meeting and ask anything that you need to figure out. The amazing thing about cross country coaches is that they are the most helpful and sharing coaches out there. It seems that the vast majority of cross country coaches understand the most important truth...everything we do is for the betterment of the kids.

The first and most important thing you should do if you are a younger or developing coach is to find yourself a mentor. Find someone that can answer questions for you, will share with you, challenge you, and help you move to the next level of coaching. You may outgrow this mentor and find another, but having someone in your corner that is there to make sure you are heading the right direction can be very important. I have mentored many coaches and my job is to help them fill in the gaps they may have, and get them thinking about improving. I was fortunate to be mentored by Steve Chavez who coached Murrieta Valley to some of the best teams of the late 90's and early 2000's in California. His passion and intensity were a great fit for my personality and he always went out of his way to share openly all of his workout plans and concepts to build his team. Steve left a legacy with many California coaches over the years and I was blessed to have him in my coaching career to help guide me as a young coach. I am the coach I am today because of his mentorship.

There are a lot of great websites on the Internet today that focus on distance running. From Milesplit to Dyestat, to local sites broken down by region or state, there are many ways to access information about cross country. Read as much as you can, watch workout videos and races, and discover potential coaches that you may want to reach out to. YouTube is another great website to utilize, from Ted Talks, to motivational videos, to race videos, there is an almost unlimited number of items to watch. I've watched every Footlocker race I could find on there, and learned a lot more about the history of our sport in the process. Set aside time to hit the Internet looking for information, motivation, and ways for you to improve your team.

There are many great books about distance running and coaching. As you move through those genres, start to think outside the box a little. Try books that discuss visualizations, warrior mentality, game strategy, and successful people. What can you take from these concepts and apply to your coaching? So much of what we do parallels coaching in other sports, or business success, or military concepts. Challenge yourself to read, but also to read books that fill in your gaps as a coach. Identify your strengths, and your weaknesses on a sheet of paper. What books can you read that will help you improve your weaknesses? What books can you read that will take your strengths to an even higher level. Remember, they don't have to be books about distance running, they have to be books that challenge you to be better at what you do.

The Power of Reaching Out to Others

Never underestimate the power of reaching out to others. Not only do other coaches out there want to share with you, but many have ideas and concepts to share with you that you didn't even know you were missing! With the power of email, you can easily email any coach in the country. Use this as an opportunity to expand your coaching network, and to find answers to problems in your coaching. None of us are perfect, we all need help and support from time to time. Build a coaching network that includes coaches both local and far away. This will allow you to share information and it will help you build a better program for your athletes.

I've had many coaches reach out to me over the years, and I always do my best to answer any questions they may have. One such example was with a newer coach who was excited about the possibility of his young team. He emailed many times, asked to see training schedules, and implemented many things I gave to him into his program. A couple seasons later, he emailed me out of the blue to let me know that his program had won their first league title in school history in cross country! Because he had the courage to ask, to incorporate, and to challenge his athletes, his team had found a level of success that they were never previously close to. In fact, when he took over, they were last in the league by a large margin! Never be afraid to ask other coaches to share info with you, and never be afraid to share with others. This is how all of us can improve our sport!

I challenge you at the conclusion of this book to identify five coaches across the country or close to home to email and ask a couple questions of. Why? Because you need to start building your coaching network, you need to get out of your comfort zone, and you need to challenge your own ideas about training and building athletes. Building a coaching network allows you to have a group of coaches to reach out to when you get stuck as a coach, and they often can help move you forward. Write down the names of coaches off the top of your head that you are interested in reaching out to. I have found that 90% of the coaches I have reached out to have not only responded, but shared anything I asked for. I can count on one hand how many coaches I know that refuse to share and support each other, and I believe that the sport will remember them that way. Be a part of the success in coaching athletes by sharing with others.

The great thing about reaching out is that you may find your mentor. You may build friendships that last a lifetime. This is your homework assignment, start reaching out and building a coaching network!

Using Social Media to Connect with Other Coaches

Since about 2009, the majority of us have been walking around with a smart phone in our pockets. These smart phones are a solution to a very fundamental problem, reaching out to coaches far away. Of course, you can email, but a much faster way to make connections with coaches that you don't know personally and may never meet is to reach out to them on social media. Tweet at them, or send them a DM. Follow them and ask questions. Congratulate them. Above all, share your team and your thoughts, and often you will find that other coaches will reciprocate that.

There are a lot of social media platforms to choose from,

and in some ways, you should be on all of them. I'm not, and probably won't ever be, but I do my best to do a great job with the ones I am on, so that I can maximize the outcomes on them. I prefer Twitter, direct news straight to me about what I'm interested in, and easy to share a thought. Instagram is currently where most of the kids are, so that is a great place to share concepts with your team. Facebook is where most parents are, so I avoid that like the plague, but we use it. I have my booster moms troll it for me, keeping an eye out for useful information, and sharing team activities. For other social media, I may ask athletes to keep an eye out for information on other teams or athletes, even though I'm not going to download those apps for me, I still have feelers out.

Utilize social media to make connections with other coaches by sharing your team culture, activities, successes, and areas your looking to improve. By simply putting out that you need advice, many coaches will share their thoughts with you. Don't overthink it, utilize it in some way to connect.

Clinics

I have attended many clinics as a coach trying to learn, and presented at many more. What I have always found is the level of collegiality at clinics is second to none. The coaches that are there are all in share and learn mode, with tons of questions being asked and many people thinking about answers to them. What clinics have you been to? I would recommend that a coach goes to 3-4 clinics a year, focusing on learning a couple new things at each one they can take back to their team and try out.

There are a lot of great national level clinics, like the Boulder Running Clinic in Colorado every January, hosted by Colorado Buffalo alum and author Jay Johnson. These larger clinics often have three or more of the best coaches in the country in attendance, and 200+ coaches in the audience. Sometimes the friendships you make in the audience are the best part of the clinic. For me, the clinics often tear down the walls we build up during competition, and allow us to reach out to other coaches to learn from them. No matter how successful you have been, no matter how much you think you know, there is always something to learn. I highly recommend going to a big clinic and getting that experience!

Find smaller, more localized clinics as well. Go with a goal of meeting a couple new coaches, and seeing someone that you haven't heard speak before. I love going to a clinic and getting the training of other coaches. How did they put their training schedule together? Are they doing something I should be doing? Does their schedule confirm how I train athletes, or challenge everything we do? I like to go into a clinic with a list of questions I have for the speakers if I know anything about their program. I'm there to get answers, and I do my best to make sure to ask the questions that need to be answered. Don't be afraid to raise your hand and ask the "dumb" question. Often, the rest of us are thinking it too. If you don't have any clinics in your area, start one!

Utilizing Message Boards

I know, I know, message boards? Really? YES! The most famous of the message boards out there is letsrun.com, but there are many others that are local or developing on the Internet that you can utilize to communicate your thoughts and questions to other coaches.

5 Reasons to Utilize a Message Board

1. Connect with the general consensus of what is going on in the country or locally.

2. Connect with other coaches.

3. Rumors. Who is healthy, who is injured, and who is having issues? These rumors can help when it comes to race planning!

4. Share your thoughts. Some will hate you for it, but

conversely, some will want to join your coaching network, as they think like you do.

5. Rankings. Yes, rankings abound, but often message boards will know about transfers, improvements, and incoming 9th graders that the media hasn't heard about yet.

PART III: PERFECTING AND MAINTAINING AN ELITE CULTURE

The culture of a program, whether good or bad, tends to show through to the other teams you are around. You can tell the teams that are just out there to have fun, the ones that have all the smart kids at the school and running is very secondary, the ones that want to be good and try hard but just don't really know how to put it all together, and the teams that have figured it out.

Football coach Chip Kelly was quoted as saying "Culture beats scheme." I've always taken this to mean that in the short run a scheme or concept that someone comes up with may find a way to win, but to be successful long term, you need to build a culture that benefits everyone on your team. Everyone has to be working towards the same goals, and believing in them at a level that makes them a possibility. We often face different teams each year at state. It is Great Oak versus whoever has put it together that year. That is how we know our culture is working, we are always battling for the title, but it is almost always against someone different.

I've often been asked what our culture is in our program. The truth is we haven't defined it as much as we just live it. It is World Domination. It is a culture of winning, and of expectation. It is a culture that thrives off of working hard, and finding a way to include every athlete on the quest towards being the best version of themselves that they can be. I will tell the athletes on my team that I'm more worried about them giving their best than them being a great runner. I'll take a 24:00 5k guy all day if he has the heart of a champion. Some of the hardest working kids I've ever coached had no talent at all, but they cared about the team and lived the culture. Those athletes make it all worth it. In 2013, senior Jeremy Stumpp defied the odds and made our top 7 for the state meet. He was very slow as a frosh when he joined us, in fact most of the frosh girls were considerably faster than he was. He bought into the culture 100%. He was going to be the best runner he could be. He worked hard, used summer and winter base building, and was just happy to have the chance to compete. Each season he got a little better, and a little more competitive. There is no doubt that Jeremy earned his spot at state. On our team, nothing is given, but it was amazing to see someone who really didn't have that athletic gift buy into the culture of our program and end up on the line for us at state. Define a culture where anyone who believes has a chance of realizing that dream.

Part of the reason we haven't defined our culture is because it isn't static, it is dynamic and ever changing. How can culture remain the same over years with different clientele? The athletes change, the assistants change, the accomplishments change, the leaders change, so the culture will have to evolve as well. Some of our best years culture wise were years ago, we may never reach that cultural pinnacle again, but we will build the best culture we can with who we've got now. Everyone on your team should be able to identify the components of your culture, but be careful of being so rigid that they don't have the ability to grow past and expand your culture. Motivational speaker and author Eric Thomas articulates that you should look "to be able, at any moment, to sacrifice what you are, for what you will become." Athletes and coaches need to be prepared to move their culture to another level when the opportunity presents itself. Statements like "this is how we have always done it" and "we don't do it like that here" show a rigid approach to culture. It shows that only things that make the people in charge comfortable will be tolerated. Sometimes you have to step out of your comfort zone or be willing to allow your athletes to step out of theirs to find and grow the next level of the culture of your program. Don't fear change, fear a lack of leadership. That starts with you.

A major part of our culture defining for the following season comes at our May Top 16 Meeting, where the athletes define their goals and what changes they believe need to occur for the betterment of the program. Make sure they you have a hand on the reigns of your program, but that the athletes also have the opportunity to affect change. When the athletes know that they aren't fighting you for control of culture, but building it with you, you can create something truly special.

What is the difference between an average culture, a good culture, and an elite culture? Can those concepts even truly be defined? How do you even know what level of culture you have? How do you value winning and why? As you outline the culture for your program, leave room for input from assistants and athletes. You set the foundations, but allow for everyone to have input on what the final product will look like. Let's take a look at why winning matters.

CHAPTER NINE: WORLD DOMINATION – WHY WINNING MATTERS

There is a rumor going around that winning doesn't matter. Just joining and being a part of the team is what truly matters. Caring too much about winning makes you a bad person or someone who is overzealous. The truth is that teaching others how to win, and how to win the right way is an invaluable skill that they will be able to use in all facets of life.

Why else do we play the game? Sports are an outlet for the energy that historically was used to fight wars. If we are going to take that energy and apply it to athletics, then this is our war! This is the fight that we have signed up for! Why in the world would we sign up for a team and act like it doesn't matter. It matters. You are creating your army, and you should be honing their skills to be the most prepared, best trained, mentally disciplined army on the battlefield at any point in time. Yes, winning matters. It teaches people how to be successful, how to strategize to get the most out of yourself, and how to deal with adversity. Yes, we want to play the game right. Yes, we want to be good sports and teach sportsmanship. Yes, we want everyone on the team to have value, but those should be the underlying tenets that your team is built upon. Those should be the pillars that your army and strategy know so innately, that they don't even have to think about them. Those concepts are on autopilot, so that the part of the brain that is designed for attack mode on race day is unfettered and ready to be unleashed.

One of the worst things you can do as a head coach is celebrate someone for doing nothing. Trophies for all kids, participation ribbons, senior nights, and all that garbage is designed to not hurt anyone's feelings. Have you ever been given the best GPA award on a team? The most likely to smile award? Does that make you feel like you contributed to the success of the team, contributed to the whole reason you were out there? Did it make you want to strive to be better, or did it pacify you to remain average? Teach every athlete on your team what they need to do to create value for themselves and for the team. Show them the best ways that they can contribute, don't pacify them. ***Don't let them feel like they accomplished something just because they showed up.*** Showing up is the base expectation. Don't reward people for breathing.

Every athlete on your team has a purpose and it is your responsibility to figure out what that is. With large teams that isn't always easy, but it is important. Teach your athletes to contribute in some way. You may not be the fastest runner on the team, but you can scream the loudest, you can lead, you can carry the team equipment so the top athletes don't have to. Teach the athletes on the team to find some way to help the team win. I've had athletes that weren't great runners, but they were amazing recruiters! They would sign up 9th grader after 9th grader and help keep them out. Some kids are amazing at fundraising at bring in a lot of money for the team. Find and expand the value of each athlete you coach. They may not be amazing athletes, but they will be a part of the winning, they can be a part of helping. That is what World Domination is. Finding the best in your athletes and teaching them how to contribute to the overall success of the team.

Defining Our Team Moto "World Domination"

Coach Daniel Noble actually started our team using the term "World Domination" in a funny animation that he put into one of our pre-race PowerPoints, and it just kind of stuck. The athletes on the team embraced the mantra as a challenge to win big at meets and to show that we weren't afraid of any of the teams that were there.

As the phrase took on life in our program, it began to define the larger scope in our program. It really meant that we would build and expect to win at all levels. That means if we go to an invitational, we are trying to win the frosh race, the soph race, the JV race, and the varsity race for both genders (or whatever races are offered). The most fun meets for our team are when we sweep the meet, and pull in the top prize for every race! To the onlooker, we can appear selfish, and not wanting anyone else to win. In reality, we are really just looking at this as an opportunity for every athlete on the team to have importance that day. Winning the frosh race at that meet is just as big of a deal as winning the varsity race. All athletes play some role and all athletes know they are important to our overall success. In a culture where only winning varsity matters, many athletes are left out of the success and often feel neglected. World Domination has evolved to mean that we want all our current, future, and former athletes to find success in their competitions and we will celebrate them! Whether it is a future Wolfpack runner doing well in middle school, a current team winning for us at an invitational, or an alum doing well at the collegiate or professional level, it is all a part of our World Domination culture, and we all celebrate those athletes' successes as if they were our own.

The best way to build depth on a roster, is not forgetting the mid and bottom level athletes on your team. Every single athlete has the ability to contribute in some way, your job is to make their contributions valuable so that they stick with your sport. We have had over 230+ athletes on a team in the past, for a sport that only really allows you 7 and 7 for varsity (per gender). That means we have to find many ways to plug those other athletes into the culture, into the success, and into the work ethic of our team.

Grade level races are a great way to start plugging athlete's in. When presented with the chance at invitationals to run more than one varsity team, take that opportunity. Why? Because you will move up 7 athletes and everyone else will now have a bigger role in the lower level races than they did before. Find ways for all your athletes to matter, which often happens in the entry process. As the head coach, put together a varsity squad made up of 9th and 10th graders and let them see what they can do. I've often put 7 frosh athletes in varsity races, so they can feel what they are working towards. It works, and also helps athletes understand why they must work harder to get to that level. World Domination is getting every athlete you are currently coaching to the best they can possibly be, while supporting athletes from years past as they test themselves at all levels, college and beyond.

Setting the Tone for Your Team

The actions of the coach go a long way to set the tone for the team. The head coach is not the sole proprietor of this responsibility, but it usually will come from them. Setting the tone on a cross country team is really about setting the expectations you want to see from your athletes emotionally, physically, and even spiritually on a daily basis throughout the season. If you set a tone of fun over work, you will probably have a lot of happy kids that are out there to be a part of the journey, but that don't really care about the results. If you define results over everything, then you may lose a lot of the athletes that have talent, but don't want to be on a team that is all work and no play. You have to find a way to define an attitude that results are fun, running is what we want to do to get results, and the social aspect will have its moments throughout the season.

Elite championship teams often have a ton of fun, they

just know when to have it. Fun doesn't have to be horseplay at practice. It doesn't have to be consistently a part of the fabric of your team. *Fun is the result you get when you are doing everything else right.* Winning meets is fun! Traveling as a team is fun! Doing pasta parties, beach parties, team dances is fun! As the head coach, your job is to set the tone that both work and fun are an awesome part of your program, just at the right and appropriate times.

Setting the tone with assistant coaches is also important. Show them that you want them to understand that the program comes first. It comes before power, decision making, and looking good. Train your assistants to execute the team plan, to stay on the road map. Empower them to do great things, but in the confines of the team plan and goals. Let them know you are there to support them, but give them guidelines to that support. At the end of the day, assistants are there to support the team vision and the head coach. Make sure they know that.

Setting the tone with parents can be very difficult when you are a beginning coach, and a lot easier when you are successful one. As a beginning coach, you need to do research and outline realistic expectations for your athletes, and for your parents. I have always found that giving my parents something to do, giving them a stake in the success, helps a lot in building trust and support between parents and the coaching staff. The majority of parents want to see two things; that their child succeeds and that their child is enjoying the journey. When you set up your road map for a season, think about how those two items can be met, and you will run into very few issues with parents. Also, spend time getting to know your parent's skill sets. If they can build, awesome! Now you have someone to build you plyo boxes. If they are a techie, great! Now you have someone to film or help you with emails or websites. If they are lawyer, buddy up with them and they will be there to help you with advice when you need it. Parents can be one of the best things to ever happen to you if you let them. Sometimes I miss the parent more than I miss their kid!

Setting the tone with administration, is different in every building. I have had principals that loved me, supported my programs, and enjoyed our success. I've had a few that did not. In today's age, we go through principals and assistant principals quickly in many areas. The first thing your admin should think about you is that you have it together, you get things done. The second thing is that you want to do the work, not them. You will set your schedule, provide bus leave times, and coordinate with the athletic secretary. If you want your admin to work with you, show them you are the hardest working coach on their coaching staff.

Setting the tone with your peers can be easy for some, and difficult for others. Personality plays a very big role in this, but I will tell you that your road map should drive your decisions, not the fear of what others may think of you. Never make decisions because you think it will make you popular, or because you think it won't. Make decisions that are in the best decision of your program and you won't ever have to explain them to anyone. Find the coaches that you work well with, network, build relationships, but never forget that you are competing against them. This year you might be better than them, but 3 years from now, that can flip-flop. I liken this to sitting at a poker table and talking to the people around you. Some butter you up, some put in headphones and wear sunglasses, and some don't stop talking to the whole table. All have an angle, and it is to take your money. Same thing applies with questions you get from your peers. They want to know what you do so they can formulate how to beat you. Keep the important things close to the vest. Remember that during competition, you are not out there to make friends, that is a side effect of working hard and building a great team!

Championship Mindset

A championship mindset is the internal understanding that every single step you are taking towards a certain point in time, has a purpose and meaning behind it, to affect a specific championship outcome. Many of the best athletes in history had tremendous championship mindsets, from Steve Prefontaine to Michael Jordan. Some people are wired this way, but many of your athletes are not. You will be the one who will need to rewire their brains over the course of time to get them focused like a championship athlete, working to help win a team championship.

What are the pieces of a championship mindset in our program? Consistency? Focus? Dedication? Drive? Desire? The will to win? I like to look at each one of my varsity athletes and try to determine their strengths and weaknesses. Why will this kid be on the line for me when it matters? What do they have internally that will get them to the line when we need it? Talent? Talent only gets you on the line, it is the championship mindset that produces when it matters. Destiny Collins was always mentally ready for state, I didn't have to try to get her there, she was wired to compete against the best. Identify the areas your team is the weakest, and spend a lot of time trying to develop that part of your team during practice. Identify the athletes that have a championship mindset, and fast track them towards your top 7. Those are the athletes that will win you championships.

Compete in Practice!

I have often been amazed at how many coaches openly admit that they don't like to have their athletes compete in practice! Who better to help you sharpen your competitive toolset than the people you already have access to? Have times for competition written into your training plan. Let them know there will be times to compete and show what you can do, and times to just focus on specific paces.

Time trials are a great way to compete in practice. In late summer, put your athletes into specific teams and hold a race. It can be as simple as a mile, but letting athlete's blow off a little of their competitive juices can allow them to learn in a safe and controlled environment. I've found athletes in practice that hadn't shown anything amazing until we started to compete. Don't hold your athletes back from competing, instead harness that competitive build up and release it when you most need it.

Another great way to build team competition in a fun way is to get three volunteers from each grade level and give them something to compete at. Most crunches, push-ups, or who can hold a plank for a set amount of time, can be fun ways to engage not only the athlete in the arena, but their supporters on the sidelines cheering them on. I love to have the winning team choose the activity for the losing grades. I give them one easy task (30 Jumping Jacks), one medium task (40 Push-ups), and one difficult task (60m lunges) to choose from. It is amazing to watch the athletes' debate whether they should be nice or mean to their teammates. Usually the pick something pretty easy, but every once in a while, you get a group that is merciless. The athlete's that lose never forget it either, and when it is their turn, they will repay the favor in kind. Usually smiles all around in these competitions though.

Our athletes often compete in our HIIT routines, although that isn't their specific function, I do use those as a chance to challenge our athletes to be better than they think they can be.

Ultimately, teaching your athletes to compete in practice means they will be ready for competition when the gun goes off for real. Michael Jordan went hard at his teammates every single day. How did that pay off? 6 NBA Championships. Compete.

Winning Leads to More Winning!

Winning can almost start to feel like you are running downhill while everyone else is on the flat ground. Once your athletes, coaches, and parents have a taste of winning, they will crave more and often start making the sacrifices it takes to make it a reality. In our program, winning is a foundational expectation. Why else do we compete as a team than to try to win the race? Obviously, there are many great side effects of competition, but those aren't the reason that we compete. We line up to see who is the best, that is why everyone gets a place and every team gets a score. We want to know who the champion is!

I've often told my teams that if they can win at such a high level that the other teams realize they will never get to that level, then you will have beaten them for good. You won't have to go all out the next time, because they already know you are going to beat them. I've had other coaches walk into our stadium waving a white flag, literally letting me know they aren't going to try. Often teams won't put their best athlete's out against us because they already know the result, and they don't want their top athletes to get discouraged. The beauty for me as a coach? I no longer have to run my top kids in a lot of meets to still be successful. We have won so definitively in the past, that many teams are already running for second, regardless of who I put out on the line to race them. I'm not saying you must break every team you face, but if you can identify the ones that you want to break so you can go easier against them in the future...that can pay off big time.

Winning creates a momentum of its own. Utilize that momentum. Even at the younger grade levels I've seen athlete's not want to lose a frosh race because we haven't lost one in a while and they don't want to be the weak link. Recognize when you have a group of athletes that is motivated by the successes they are having, and put them in situations to continue that winning momentum. Often, these athletes will become some of the best in your program, because they crave the feeling of winning.

As you build your seasonal road map, think about how you can start the season off with 3 or 4 wins. Put together a schedule that builds momentum towards the end of the season, one where your athletes are having fun and ready for more. When the athletes on your team can't stop talking about the next pit stop on the road map, you know you have built momentum towards something good going forward. Utilize it!

Cross Country Game Theory

To the passive observer, cross country is a basic sport. Kids line up, they race, and the results speak for themselves. As a head coach, your job is to do everything that you can to turn the math in your favor so that your results are better than everyone else's. Understanding the ability of your team, with what you believe everyone else in the race can do, gives you the ability to formulate a strategy for winning the race.

How do you turn the math in your favor? The easiest way to do that is to utilize all seven runners. Your goal is to create a team that has the depth to always give you seven elite level capable performances so that at any point and time you can get five amazing finishes to win races. Everyone gets a couple talented athletes, but it is the coaches that develop athletes that have the depth to put out teams that can consistently win. If you are competing against a team that has three superstars and a couple decent runners, your advantage isn't in trying to beat them at the front, it is in making sure you destroy them at the four and five positions. Teams with five really good runners but not a lot of depth can't afford to have one off race by any of those five athletes. Teams that have seven good runners can take five good races by any of the seven and most likely win, which creates a major advantage going into large invitationals and championship races. This is why creating depth on your team is the ultimate consistency factor there is. The deeper your team, the more consistently you will win meets over a sustained period of time.

Growing up my dad taught me how to play poker when I was 5 years old. He would give me my allowance and play me poker for it. He would let me get up big so I would feel good and then encourage me to take the money off the table and walk away up. Of course, as a kid you feel like you are winning easily so you keep pushing your luck, and he would take it all back and I would end up broke. The lesson he was teaching me was learning how to stop when you had what you needed out of the game. In cross country there are always opportunities to push more, run more mileage, run faster. As a coach you have to master when to back off, when to quit, and when to make modifications. You can't just push through every scenario full steam ahead; you have to know when enough is enough. You learn how to read your team like a poker player reads the other players. Sometimes you just have to shut down a workout because you have accomplished what you needed to accomplish, no need to keep pushing.

Poker is a game that to be successful, you have to read the other players and adjust probability on the fly. Learning poker at a young age taught me to read the people I'm interacting with. What is their agenda? What are they trying to get out of this? How do I need to play this to get this athlete to do what we need them to do for us all to be successful? Poker teaches you to understand the value of the bets you are making, and as a coach that helps you understand the risk vs. reward of making any decision. Your job is to make better decisions than your peers do on a consistent basis. If you can do that, you can up your odds of winning as a head cross country coach by a large percentage.

When I first graduated from college and moved to Palm Springs, California to begin teaching and coaching, I switched up my poker playing from home games to tournament poker in the local casinos. When I first began playing, I was 24 years old and usually the youngest player at the table by 30+ years. The old timers loved pulling moves on me that nobody else at the table would fall for, but I was quick to adapt. When you can hold your own against a pack of wolves, you learn there is no competitive situation that you can't prepare for, there is no reason to be afraid of intense competitive situations. You learn how to handle pressure, and you learn that when someone tries to pull a move on you, you need to be steps ahead and ready to catch them in a trap. I learned to see it coming a mile away and set the trap for them. Sitting at a poker table in poker tournaments taught me how to survive rounds, how to know when to push and when to sit back, and how to develop an advantage by being more prepared and ready than my opponents. Tournaments are about knowing how to survive, when moves should be made, need to be made, or should be avoided at all costs. Translating this to coaching, this same strategy applies to defining the strategy of surviving the rounds you face during the post season. To be an elite coach, you have to know how to get your athletes through league, sectionals, and state using the least amount of effort and resources possible so that you can compete at nationals as fresh, focused and prepared as possible.

I've always been a competitor and loved games growing up as a kid. Chess, Stratego, Risk, Monopoly, Poker, and eventually the Magic the Gathering card game filled my days. Each one of these games forces you think about forming a strategy for winning and slowly refining it as you find out what works and what doesn't. It gives you an opportunity to learn how to dominate your opponents. I spent hour upon hour formulating Magic card decks, looking at every probability and outcome based on the cards I was choosing to put in the deck. I wanted to know that I was going to win before we ever started a match. This was fun for me, but the people I played against quickly decided it was better for them to move on to other things. They simply weren't willing to put in the time to understand how to counter my strategies. I was willing to spend hours to not only win, but to win in a way that made their deck essentially worthless. You can do the same thing in coaching, but you have to be willing to put in the time and understand that it won't make you popular with the other coaches.

What strengths do you have that you have gained along the way? What skills are you missing that you need to improve through study? Identify your weaknesses, because understanding what makes you vulnerable gives you a chance to fill that hole, that gap in your armor that someone can get through. Figure out what you need to do to move to the next level to compete with coaches that have advantages over you.

CHAPTER TEN: OFFERING A BETTER PRODUCT – HOW TO CONVINCE ATHLETES TO FOLLOW YOU

Would you rather eat an expensive steak or have a simple hamburger? This is really the choice you are offering your athletes every time they are with you. Is your program the steak, or is it the hamburger? Many times in my career I have recruited a great frosh runner that just happened to be very good at another sport. Now every coach has a different philosophy towards athletes playing multiple sports, but I have always believed that if you want to build aerobic athletes, you must consistently be building the aerobic component, which doesn't give you time for seasons off to play other sports. When a good soccer player, or Irish Dancer, or baseball player join our squad, I will always try to evaluate them as a runner versus their other passion. If they are better or have a better long term outlook in the other sport, I encourage them to focus there. If they are a better runner, then I try to show them why they need to be a part of our program year round, and that the sacrifices that they make will determine the outcomes that they get as a runner.

In 2008, I ended up with a little brother of one of my

varsity girls from our early years named Karson Fronk. I believe he first came out because his sister ran and his parents wanted him to give it a try, but his first love was basketball! His freshman year he ran cross country, then went to basketball, then came out for track and eventually ended up injured. Sophomore year, pretty much the same thing happened. At the end of his soph season I sat down with him and asked him what he wanted to accomplish as a runner, and he told me that he wanted to be one of the best milers in California. I told him that he would be, if he gave up basketball. He looked at me with an intensity that I will never forget. He wasn't upset, but he was calculating whether or not giving up his dream of basketball was worth becoming a top miler, and whether or not I could get him there. In the end he made the commitment. As a junior, his training improved tremendously with the consistency he had gained. He leaned up, as there was no more demand for the muscle he wanted to put on for basketball. He started breaking 4:20 in his 1600's, and he started winning races. Not only dual meets, but also invitationals, against big name athletes. By the time he was a senior, he was confident and ready going into every meet. He had completely bought into his dream of becoming a top level miler, and worked extremely hard to develop his last lap speed. He had a tremendous senior year, culminating in a 7th place finish at the California State Track & Field Meet in the 1600, and a win in the mile at the Nike Track Nationals! Prove yourself as a coach, and athletes will follow you.

There are many ways to offer a better product than your competitors in club or the other sports on your campus. Traveling, gear, making varsity early in their careers, and the ability to be on a close knit team are just a few examples of ways you can create a better place for athletes to be than where they initially believe themselves headed when they come into your school. I've found that being nice to athletes versus yelling at them tends to tip the balance our way against many club soccer coaches with European accents.

Travel Trips

When I started the program at Great Oak in 2004, my goal was to build a nationally competitive program. One of the best ways to do that is to travel and compete against the best in the nation and see how you stack up. We have traveled to New York, North Carolina, Minnesota, Texas, Idaho, Oregon, and Arizona to take on some great teams. I believe that this travel has been a huge reason why we have been able to get some of the top athletes on our campus to come out for cross country at Great Oak.

I've often been asked why I think traveling across the country in the middle of the season makes sense. One of the main reasons I believe in it is that it gives our program the opportunity to see teams on their courses, with their advantages, putting us at a disadvantage. There is nothing like stepping into hostile territory and taking on teams where they have all the advantages and want to show this team from California that they are better than we are. It gets us great competition, but it bonds us and helps us form an **identity** for that season!

Travel trips that the athletes have a hand in selecting go a long way in giving your athletes something to look forward to between the start of training and the end of the season. It allows you as a coach to break up the season into smaller goals leading to the bigger goals at the end of the season. I've always said we can't lose on these trips, if someone beats us, we find out what we need to work on for the post season, and if we win, we build confidence for the remainder of the year. No matter what, the kids have fun and make memories and I get to offer them a better product than the club soccer coaches that are trying to keep them from running for me.

Everything we do in our program is in some way related to being prepared for the California State Cross Country Meet in

November. When we travel, we are preparing for the same types of things that they will experience on that state trip, and the better prepared they are, the more ready they will be on race day. I like to have my kids traveled to the point that going to state or NXN is just another stop on the road map, and not some super exciting event. If state is off the charts exciting for your team, the odds are that it is also off the charts scary. We want it to be just another race, albeit one that they are very, very prepared for.

Gear

Sponsorships are hard to come by, and the amazing shoes, clothes, and uniforms that can come along with them can be a big draw for athletes trying to decide between one sport or another. Our programs have been sponsored by New Balance and most recently Nike. The beauty of working with a company like Nike is that they can help you develop a vision for your team, and can help that vision evolve as your team does. What GO wore in 2009 is vastly inferior to what we wear now. Basic off the shelf uniforms have been replaced by consistent sets of originally designed custom uniforms. It didn't come easy and it wasn't quick, but it was something that has paid off for our program.

From 2004-2013 we were wanting to be sponsored, but had not done enough at the national level to get noticed. In 2014, New Balance became our sponsor and upped our look for us that season. The following year, we switched over to Nike and have formed a partnership that has allowed our athletes and coaches to design a custom look for our team each season, giving us a distinct advantage not only over most of our competitors, but also the other teams on our campus. Our extra warm-ups have even been purchased by other teams on our campus, because our team is always in the newest and the best gear. It isn't easy to get sponsored by a team, and the best way is to show that you are consistently going to be in contention on the national level.

Our team colors are red, white, and navy blue, so designing a custom look for the elites on our team requires going outside the basic. To create custom gear that everyone on the team wanted to work towards, that only went to the elite athletes on the team, we had to go outside of the average color scheme and design in blacks, greys, and other colors that the average athletes on the team didn't have. Always give your athletes something to work towards! Always push the envelope of cool, knowing that it is an ever changing concept. Believe me, your athletes have a better idea of current fashion than you do. Have them help!

Don't Forget to Have Fun!

At the end of the day, if you aren't enjoying yourself out on the field, then you have to ask yourself why you do it. To build a team, the athletes have to have some fun somewhere along the way. One time I spent a lot of our practices with my freshman at the start of the season, and kept talking about how much fun the sport was. After one difficult portion the frosh group was sitting down waiting for the last few kids to finish when one of the girls asked me, "Coach Soles, when does it get fun?" Not everyone will see practice or running as a super enjoyable time, especially at first, and you need to get them to buy in to the full season to see some of the fun things you do.

Mammoth Camp – There probably isn't an event that our kids look forward to more outside of meets, than our yearly trip to Mammoth. We do focus on goal setting, but we spend a lot of our time getting to really know each other. We have done music festivals, hikes to Devil's Post Pile Monument and Rainbow Falls, scavenger hunts, team movie nights, and bowling while at camp. Utilize this time to ratchet up the fun, all in the name of team bonding!

Color Wars Week is designed as a fun introduction to team cross country. We put our athletes into a Red, White, or Blue team and hold a week full of competitions, culminating in a frosh 1 mile race at the end of the week. The older varsity athletes are their coaches, and it gives the 9th graders a great chance to learn about team cross country, while building a passion for our team and their teammates. We usually hold this in late August as we prep for the upcoming racing season.

For as long as I can remember coaching, we have done the Dana Hills Beach Party. We take the whole team to a really early meet over at the beach in Dana Point at Dana Hills High School. It is a flat fast course and usually produces a lot of PR's. After the meet, we head down to the beach area and the parents throw us a big party for about 4 hours. The kids go nuts and play at the beach, eat tons of food, and just generally have a good time. This trip is a highlight for many because everyone gets to go and all the barriers of who is varsity and who is JV or frosh melt away. We just all have a good time together, which is great for team bonding.

We came up with our team event, the Neon Dance, at camp one year. The kids were dancing like crazy at the little outdoor mall up in Mammoth, because a DJ was playing for everyone outside. Seeing how much fun they had, we decided to create a dance event for our team during the season as a way to have fun and blow off steam after a race. We have everyone dress up in neon and white clothing and bring in a DJ and ton of food and activities. The team loves it and votes to keep it in our schedule each season. I highly recommend finding an activity like this for fun and team bonding.

In our program, we get a chance to travel a lot in a season. We have the Mammoth Camp trip, usually an early season overnight meet for 56 selected athletes, a varsity top 7 only elite meet that we take the elite athletes to (Manhattan, Great American, Bob Firman, etc.), the Clovis Invite where we bring another 56 athletes for development on the state meet course, and State and Nike Cross Nationals. Travel trips give your athletes experience traveling and competing, and something to look forward to. We treat them as a business trip, but also find ways to have a good time. Know when to dial them in, and when to let them be relaxed and enjoy the adventure. I highly recommend all teams have at least one big travel trip each season!

Why Picking the Right Schedule is Important?

Your kids love to compete! Some of them just don't know it yet. For most athletes the meets will be the most fun part of the season. Put together a schedule that allows the varsity to compete, grow, and develop for championships season, while still allowing all the other athletes on the team to have fun and gain some race experience. Although our top varsity athletes only compete 4-5 times total during the regular season on our team, our younger athletes and junior varsity athletes will pretty much attend every race.

The early meets of the season are all about the frosh on the team in my opinion. It is fresh and new, and getting a chance to see what talent lies in your latest group is a lot of fun for coaches. If you have superstars in your 9th grade group, give them chances to win grade level races, but it is ok to slip them into varsity races from time to time too, to get a feel for what it may feel like later on down the line. The first meet of the season is a chance to bring in, build up, and expand your team culture with your younger kids.

Picking a schedule that lends itself to the right amount of competition, with a little bit of fun mixed in is usually the right way to go. Since our athletes pick a lot of our schedule, it is my job to make sure they have a good idea what meets are available and the pros and cons of each of those meets they might pick. You can tell a lot about your team by the schedule they push for. All fun and games and you know they are more worried about the experience than the mission. Every meet is top tier and they may not be factoring in the younger kids on the team, but may be very focused on winning. Give your team a chance to pick some of the meets you attend, and make sure some of them are "highlight" meets that your athletes are looking forward to during the journey.

Teach race day preparation, so when you get to the post season, they are so prepared, you won't have to say a word. By the time your athletes make it to their bigger meets, you have programed them to know what to eat, how to mentally be prepared for their races, when to warm-up, how to warm-up, and how to be race ready. Use the regular season as your trial and error period. Stomach hurt during the race? What did you eat or drink? Find the problems for each athlete and have them ready in every department come championship season. This is another reason why travel is so important with your team, they can't be excited to stay in a hotel on a trip, they need to be used to it. Teach them to lock in what works and eliminate what doesn't for them on race day.

Lack of Money Doesn't Stop You!

In 2004 I accepted the job at Great Oak with the mindset that we were going to compete against the best teams in the nation. To do that you need to travel and go to the best meets each season, so you better have some money in your parent booster account to be able to pull that off. Now I know what you are thinking, Great Oak has all kinds of money but your program comes from an area that does not. In the early years of us traveling, I told the athletes to dream big and to leave it to me to find a way to make it happen. There were a few sleepless nights, but when you put yourself out there like that, you will force yourself to deliver. We took two trips to the Manhattan Cross Country Invitational in the Bronx, New York. I still don't know how we paid for those trips, but I know that they were critical in the long term success of our program. Athletes were committing themselves at very high levels at a chance to make the big trip with our team. By dangling that carrot, we got paid back in gold by hordes of excited runners looking to prove themselves for an opportunity to go on next year's trip!

What happens if you go to a small school or a poor school, or a rural school without many resources or support? The truth is YOU are the person who must create those resources and build that support. Parents, alumni, local businesses, athletes extended family members, and anyone else you can think of are where you start building your network of support. It can be as simple as having your kids run coupons out to all the houses in the area to support the local pizza shop, and they in turn donate some money to the program. The kids get a workout, and you get a little extra money to build with. Be creative, think outside the box. Find the rich guy in town and convince him that supporting the cross country team will make him look smart and great. Put his name on your team website or name a weekly award after him. Look at this guy, he is amazing! More money for your program. My first program was as poor as can be. I would buy all the closeout spikes I could with my own money so that the kids would have spikes in track. I'd sell them to the kids for a buck and make sure everyone had what they need. The only thing that stops you is your imagination. Make your program a way out of the small town for your athletes.

Fundraising strategies – If your team has numbers, do an email fundraiser, car wash, food nights at the local restaurant, trip ticket raffle, and an iPhone or iPad raffle. Find great parents and put them in charge. Big teams have it easy, where smaller teams will need to be more creative and may have to look outside of the town for support. Is there a big company in a big city nearby that wants to support the little guy? Many companies have donations they are looking to make for tax reasons, they just need help in where to put the money. The best strategy is putting together a group of 6-10 parents and giving them some guidance on what you want for fundraising. I have found that a motivated group of parents can accomplish a ton!

Winning the Battle with Club Soccer and Other Sports

When I speak at a convention, I'm often asked how to win the battle with club soccer? Many coaches want to know the answer, because all of us are affected by this in some way! The key is to offer a better product. Almost across the board the only way you have of winning the war with club soccer or any of the other sports that are pulling athletes from your program is to offer product that they will enjoy more. The athlete that is playing both sports, is going to always be in a mental tug of war with playing both, or choosing one to focus on. Have a strategy in place to up your chances of winning that battle. I will say though, if an athlete is a better soccer player than they are going to be a runner, I always encourage them to focus on soccer. I had a girl want to join xc that already had offers from many PAC-12 schools for soccer as a frosh. She was a good runner, but a great soccer player. I encouraged her not to run, but to focus on soccer. She ended up signing with a great program and it made sense for all parties involved.

To me, the number one reason athletes show up to practice isn't running, it is the *friendships* they make on the team. We have won over many athletes because our kids were just nicer and more fun to be around than the ones in the other sport. Teach this to your athletes, make sure that they understand that being a good teammate and helping to win over athletes from competing teams benefits everyone long term in our program. Work hard to connect your athletes with kids on the team that will up your chances of winning them over from their other sport.

Club soccer teams *travel*, and that is fun! What is your schedule like? Do you travel? Do you do overnight opportunities and big meets? If you don't, you are missing a big weapon in the battle for those athletes. If a club team gets to go on a few trips, some overnight, and your team is running dual meets at the local park, which one would you choose as a 15 year old? You would want to travel. Why? Because it is new and exciting! The thrill of traveling, of the unknown, of the silly inside jokes that are told, the roommates you end up being best friends with, and the adventure of something new all make being on a team that gets to travel the place to be. Weigh out what the local clubs do, and top it. They go on 2 trips; you go on 3. They travel 100 miles; you fly across the country. Choose trips that your kids really, really want to go on, and watch the club kids get really serious about running, really fast.

Gear. Gear matters. Now we have been a sponsored team by New Balance and Nike, and we have lots of great gear. I realize not everyone is going to have that option. That is ok! Sit down with your assistants, your athletes, your parents, and formulate a gear plan. What color scheme do we want to go with this season? What pieces of clothing do we need? You can create it or have a company create a custom gear shop for your families to purchase from. The key is you need to craft a custom design for each season, each year, that your athletes are excited about. Jackets, sweatshirts, headbands, socks, custom uniforms, you name it and the kids will want it. Create a custom warm-up or uniform concept that only varsity athletes can purchase. Give something for the athletes on your team to set as a goal gear wise. Every athlete wants to own the gear that signifies that they are the important ones on the team, and they will work hard to earn it! Make your gear the best on the campus and you will increase your chances of winning kids over from other sports.

Treatment. One of the easiest ways to be the team your athletes want to be at over their other sport, is the way they are treated. If their club soccer coach is always yelling at them, and you are always nice and supportive, then it really increases your chances of winning this battle. Take note of your athletes that are playing another sport, and listen for when the coach of that sport is being mean or difficult in the athlete's opinion. That is where you move in and let them know how great it is that they are on the team, and how happy you are that they are running for you. This wins over a lot of athletes, because at the end of the day, everyone wants to be treated like they are an important, wanted piece of the team. Cross country isn't a sport that requires a lot of yelling, so you have the advantage.

Follow the tips above and you will have a great chance of not only winning the battle with club soccer, but many of the other teams that are keeping athletes from your program.

Create Opportunities for Your Athletes

Once you start traveling to bigger meets, you start creating more opportunities for all the athletes in your program. Only our top 7 for each gender tends to make the biggest trips each year, but when they run well, it creates opportunities for all of the athletes on the team. Many times, a coach from an area we traveled to will contact me about an athlete that was at the meet. I often recommend many of our athletes that didn't make the trip as well and have found that often those athletes that were not on the trip may have interest in the school. Find ways to create opportunities for all of your athletes, and the athletes will put in the work to create even more!

Create opportunities for college coaches to get a firsthand look at your team and your individual athletes. Having traveled all over the country with our varsity groups, I can tell you that wherever we go for our big meet trip, we end up with a lot of college letters from coaches in that area. Competing against athletes that the college coaches are already recruiting from that region, can create some tremendous opportunities for your athletes, now that they have a chance to show how they stack up. If you have the chance to take your athletes out of state, I highly recommend it. It will create opportunities for them they didn't even know existed.

One area that the athlete really wants to get paid off is in competition. As the head coach, they want me to find them amazing races, ones that challenge them in ways they haven't even conceived of yet. It is that challenge, that change from the norm, that makes it exciting. One year we traveled to the Nike South Invitational in Texas. Now we had scouted the times going into the meet, and our athletes were not that impressed. I let them know that every area, every course is different, and the results on the clock change tremendously based on those factors that may be very different than running cross country in Southern California. We had decent races, but the big take away from the meet was how different it was racing in 100% humidity, compared to our area that is often extremely dry with limited humidity at all most months of the year. That group of athletes learned that times only mean so much, because unless you have run those courses, under those conditions, you won't really know how to compare them. Create opportunities for your athletes to find exciting races, and amazing experiences.

Media Exposure for your athletes, whether through the Internet, social media, or the good old fashion newspaper, can be very important. Helping your athlete's get their name and skillset out there can help them in the recruiting process for college, with coach's being able to search up and find out more about their potential recruit. Having positive stories out there about how hard they work, their dedication to the sport and their teammates, and their success on the course can be very helpful for college coaches who may not know much about your area and the courses you run on. It is also helpful for scholarships, public speaking, and letting other teams know how good your athletes are in a specific season. As the head coach, make sure you are utilizing the media for the good of your athletes.

CHAPTER ELEVEN: CONSISTENCY: HOW GREAT OAK WON 14 OUT OF 20 STATE CHAMPIONSHIPS IN A DECADE

We went into the decade believing we could win a state championship on the girls' side, and ended up winning eight of them, and another six on the boys. That unprecedented consistency has changed the face of California cross country, and vaulted our program to the top of the state. The trick in success though, is staying there. We haven't accidentally been successful. It hasn't been a random luck of athletes, rather a plan I have aptly named Building a Dynasty. In that plan I outline who our top sevens will be 4+ years out, which helps me to identify any weaknesses in our upcoming teams, and the athletes I must identify as critical for our programs long term success. In essence, this plan is a blueprint for our upcoming potential and the personnel we will need to build championship teams, well before many of the athletes involved have ever thought about running cross country at our school.

To always be in contention, you need to master the art of

consistency, and that is not as easy as it sounds. Week in and week out, doing what needs to be done, with a group of kids that do not always have a 6 month attention span. Everyone wants to win now; everyone wants to hit a big PR and show they are one of the best in the state. To be successful as a program, you have to make sure that everyone understands and buys into the team goals and road map, and you have to be ready for the unexpected. We know someone can get hurt, or sick, or run into an issue with Ferritin. Our goal as a team is to build the best depth in the country, so if someone goes down, the athletes that are right behind them are pretty much just as good.

Building Depth is the name of the game at Great Oak. Bringing in classes of 9th graders and getting them to fall in love with the sport is key. I always let them know right off the bat that there is a reason they are there, that there is purpose to them being on the team. They immediately get a sense that they are part of something special, not just some average after school activity. We are able to build depth by making sure every athlete on the team is hitting all of the necessary components that they need to, not only get faster, but to get stronger and more confident as a runner. We are trying to build an army, not just 5-7 fast athletes. Oversell the dream and hope that the kids that don't get on the line will get a chance at some point. It isn't easy watching girls that can break 5:00 for the 1600 not make our top 7. Depth creates opportunity, but it can create competition as well. Competition can push athletes to levels they never imagined.

Coaching Boys and Girls at high level is something special. As a coach, you have to be able to understand that they are so similar, and yet so different at the same time. Boys want to go to war, they want to compete. Girls often just want to be accepted by their peers, and they want to please. Now I get that these are wild generalities and there are many that wouldn't fit those explanations, but understanding these differences as a whole has allowed me to approach the teams in similar ways in preparation, while programming them mentally in much different ways. Anyone can be successful with either gender, but you must understand that getting the buy in from either gender requires you as the coach to truly understand what drives them as a team.

Art vs. Science. For years, coaches have tried to tie down the definitions of the art of coaching versus the science behind coaching success. If you want to be elite as a coach, you better be off the charts in one of these, or pretty darn good at both. I often look at the art of coaching as the day to day interactions with athletes. It is relationship building and team activities that keep kids plugged in for the long term, while also knowing what to say to athletes when they need to hear it. The science often changes, but trying to master building a training plan, adding in things that work, and pulling out things that don't. We have been successful as a program, because we have been solid in both the art and the science of team building, and have worked to improve at both each year.

Consistently Attracting the Best Athletes

One of the main reasons Great Oak has been able to stay on top has been our success at identifying and attracting the top athletes at our school to come out and run. I don't care how good of a coach you are, how many miles you run, how much you want it, you aren't winning NXN or most likely even a state title without the horses. Talented athletes are your cornerstone, they are what you build around. That is obvious, right? I hear it often when I speak with coaches about building a team and they say they don't have enough talent to win this or that. Excuses. There is a state championship team walking the halls of almost every high school! Most schools have an NXN team walking the halls too. The truth is they are playing other sports like soccer, basketball, volleyball, etc. It is your job to get them out!

I know, I know, you can't get out every talented kid in the school. You don't have to. You have to get out that one kid. That one kid that takes your score at league from 57 to 39. That one kid that talks his buddy from soccer to also join cross country because it is fun. That one kid that loves basketball but will never be taller than 5' 7" tall. YOU have to identify the kids you can get that will make the difference in your teams' ability to compete against the best, AND you have to be a good enough coach to keep them with you!

There are lots of ways to get athletes to come out and give it a try, but the best way to get the elite athletes is to offer them a better product than what they can get somewhere else. Many of the athletes we need grow up playing club soccer and are used to the travel, the workload, the expectation. Many don't get to compete against the best in the nation, and this is where you can win over athletes that want to see their name in lights. If they travel all over the country for club soccer and you offer them 1-2 small invitationals that are local and not against anybody good, then why would they switch? Would you? The best athletes are drawn to the best programs! Many of the best athletes I have coached were top notch athletes in another sport. It was my job to make being with us a better place to be than being somewhere else. If I have an elite athlete that I want to win over, they get my full attention. They get the elite gear. They get to travel to the big meets and take on the best in the nation. They are treated like the elite athlete that they are, even if they haven't proven themselves as a distance runner yet. My job is to get them to buy in full time, after that I can develop them to become what I know they can be.

After some of our legendary talent graduated out after the 2015 and 2016 cross country seasons, I was left in rebuild mode. I was blessed with up-and-coming talent in Fatima Cortes and Arianna Griffiths, had a few solid varsity girls returning, and the amazing Tori Gaitan moving in from Yucaipa because her parents were opening a restaurant in Temecula. I knew we were going to be good up top, but I also knew that there was going to be a gap that left us vulnerable at the state level. I had to find another elite piece to keep us at the top. I knew exactly who I needed, a girl I had missed on the previous year in Aubrie Nex. Now a sophomore, Aubrie was the piece we needed to put us over the top and keep us winning state titles and competing for podium spots at NXN. A natural runner and a very talented athlete, she made running look effortless. I knew she was the one to get us where we wanted to go.

The year prior I met with her parents and did an hour-long presentation, emailed constantly, promised her everything I could to get her to try it, and she even joined for a couple days. After those couple days though she stopped showing up and said she wasn't interested. I had struck out. Spring track, same story. Club soccer and no running. We needed her for the 2017 cross country season and she debated coming out, but in the end decided she just didn't want that pressure. I was devastated. Fortunately, the girls came together and we were able to hold on for the state title that fall.

When spring track her sophomore year came around, I had pretty much given up on the dream that she would join us. I would make comments to the girls that maybe she would come out and they would all tell me that she didn't want to do it and to find someone else. Miraculously she signed up for spring track! I was so happy and couldn't wait to get a chance to turn her into a superstar. The first day she came out to tryouts and she was running around the track with one of her friends and I called her over and thanked her for joining the team. She looked at me and smiled and said "Yeah, but I think I'm going to do pole vault." In that moment of desperation, I did the one thing I would never do, I got down on both knees and begged. I said "Please give me one season. Give me one chance to show you what this team, what this group, what I am all about. I believe you will be an amazing runner and I promise you at the end of this season if it isn't your thing, I won't ever bother you again." Now I really didn't need her in track, I needed her for the following cross country season, and I needed to get a chance to prove to her that this was her thing. Reluctantly she agreed to try distance for that season and she did really well. The second time she ran the 1600 she broke 5:20 and I knew I had found my missing piece for the following cross country season.

When the 2018 cross country sign-up time started, Aubrie was a no show and I thought the dream was probably over. A few days later though, I got a call from her and she said she had fun in track and was probably going to do xc. It took me years, but I finally got her to join the cross country team! It took her a bit of the season to adapt to the distance, but by the end of the season she had gotten the hang of it and had become the 5th runner we needed. We went on to win that state title by 4 points. We won because I had identified the piece we were missing and I went out and found a way to get her on the team for when we needed her the most. No other race, no other performance mattered. We needed that one girl, for that race, and she delivered.

Never underestimate the importance of one elite athlete on your season, and never give up on that athlete if they don't initially join your team. The elite athletes are walking the halls of your school. Identify them, invite them, and offer a better product than what they can get somewhere else so that they will be there to help you when your team needs them the most!

Mileage Growth

I believe that the fear of overtraining or running too many miles in high school cross country began in the 80's, where the common belief held by many coaches was 25-35 miles a week was enough training for high school athletes. The truth though, is that nobody knows what the right amount is to run. My general rule of thumb is to build up athletes over time, understanding that the two best ways for any athlete to improve as distance runner are to run further or to run faster. As a coach, find your "Sweet Zone" where athletes tend to run fast and improve the most in your program across the board.

There are a lot of myths and mileage shaming that happens in the distance running community. If a high school coach pushes their athlete's to be their best, then they are using them up. That is obviously a myth, but it is one that fits for most college coaches. If athletes do well at the next level, they get the credit. If they do poorly, the high school coach gets the credit. The own both sides of the coin, how can they lose? The truth is however, had any of the athletes I've coached to tremendous success stayed with me the following year, keeping to their normal training, they would have continued to improve. So why do athletes fail when they move on? The number one reason is transition. Anytime you transition from one program to another, one training plan to another, an athlete can go from feeling great as a runner, to not feeling strong or confident at all. The second obvious reason is that they are making the transition from a child to an adult, and all that comes with that. They are doing things in college, making adult decisions, that they didn't have to make in high school. How can that not have an effect on their performance level? I believe we see mileage shaming of high school coaches, not because running is bad for high school kids (quite the opposite actually), but because it has developed as the easy out for why athletes don't succeed at the next level. The truth is it usually isn't the high school or college coach's fault. Often, the athlete transitions and their priorities change. Running was a way to get to college, and they see it differently now that they are there. That is part of life, and part of what will continue to happen with the way the system is set up.

It has been my observation that most top high school programs typically run anywhere from 55-80 miles a week on average during the cross country season. It is not a coincidence that the top programs also tend to run more miles than the teams they are beating. So, assuming that is true, why aren't your teams running that same mileage? The typical answers I see from coaches' land anywhere from being uncomfortable pushing the kids to they think it is too far. I think a big reason for this is that distance coaches, more than just about any other type of coach out there, get blamed for athlete's injuries. I've never heard a basketball parent or other coach say that an athlete blew out their ACL because the coach pushed them too hard. I've never heard a football parent say that the coach didn't teach their kid how to avoid tackles. There is a fear that has been created for distance coaches, that if you push an athlete hard and they get hurt, then it is your fault. To some degree it is, as you control some of the factors, but not all of them. Most coaches do not control sleep, food intake or lack thereof, or the amount of stress that is added to the student by their school work. You can run your program 35 miles a week, get good results from the really talented athletes in your program, and potentially have fewer issues with injuries or parents. You really have to decide what the team goals are. If your goals are to have fun, then let the talented athletes dominate and everyone else is what they are. If you want to be successful, you can set goals to build and develop athletes over time. To do this, you will need to build their mileage up into the 55-80 miles a week range as they get older. I'm not saying this, the data says this. The results say this.

Building up your mileage over time, to me, is a yearly thing. You start in the summer of cross country season, and build the athlete over the season. That build up should continue throughout the rest of the year. I had a girl transfer into my program and I asked her, "what mileage did you run during cross country as a frosh?" She said "35 miles a week." I asked her "what mileage did you run during the winter and during track season?" She again said "35 miles a week." Throughout an entire year's worth of training, she had not progressed at all mileage wise. Why? The coach was afraid to run a frosh more than 35 miles a week, so she stayed there and never moved. This isn't a horrible concept, because he had the athlete's best interests at heart, or at least he thought he did. In our program, we look at mileage like stairs, always working to move to the next step, or moving down a step or two if an injury strikes. So, a frosh in our program might be running 20 miles the first week of cross country practice, and 30-35 miles a week at the end of the cross country season, maybe more depending on their experience before our program. That same frosh will take a break after cross and continue to build to new highs. By the end of the track season they might be running 35-45 miles a week, and their long run may transition from 6-8 miles in cross, to 8-10 by the end of track. This stair concept continues through soph year and so on. Remember that your job is to bring them along slowly but surely, building up their strength and athleticism so that they can handle the increases in mileage.

Adjusting mileage for athletes who struggle to stay healthy is not always easy, and is part of the art of coaching. Make the right call and they have a great career. Make the wrong call and they may never get off the ground. All coaches will eventually run into the athlete that gets injured walking across the street, and when you get one of those, you have to throw everything out the window and start over. My best suggestion when dealing with athletes who struggle to build mileage, is to find what mileage they can handle, and add on EliptiGO, bike, or AlterG mileage to help them aerobically without upping their chance for injury too much. Also, spend lots of time on specific strength work around the areas they have the most trouble, and have them get custom fit for the right pair of shoes. Often, injuries are caused by imbalances and improper shoes.

The point of limited return is an important one. Why don't my athlete's consistently run 80+ miles a week? I've established that running more tends to make you faster, so why not just crank the miles? The reason is that at some point in training the athlete is breaking down at a point that they can't recover fast enough to physically be ready for the next workout. Your job as the coach is to identify that point with your athletes, and to also identify the areas you should be working on instead of adding more mileage. There are other components like plyos, HIITs, hills, med balls, etc. that you can add into your practice time to get a return that add limited to no mileage to your athlete. Every athlete is different. Find what makes sense for your program, and be aware that you may need to push some further, and some less.

Building Aerobic Athletes Instead of Distance Runners

Building an *aerobic athlete* over a distance runner is very important, because athletes have the ability to run up and down hills, kick at the end of the race at a higher level, and withstand moves made throughout a race. Many races are won in the last 400m of just about any championship distance race. Having the fastest finisher in the race can almost lock up many high school races for your athletes. You want athletes, not lungs with legs.

When you get the Bambi looking frosh coming in that don't know the difference between opposite arm and opposite leg when trying to run, you need to spend a lot of time on speed, strength, and coordination. Mileage will build over time, but it isn't the most important thing when they first come in. What you need to do is hit them with speed ladders, form drills, core strength, and plyos and med balls. You can do this stuff all day with them, and you will have the time because they aren't running very far at this point. Your goal should be to maximize the athletic ability of every athlete you get over their four years, leaving them ready to increase their aerobic ability and pacing when the move on to college.

Runners that are turned into athletes are more injury resistant, because you as the coach have spent more time on developing their core, their strength, their balance, and their overall ability than someone that focuses primarily on aerobic running. I'm not saying we don't focus aerobically, we absolutely do, but as part of the equation, not the equation itself. Ask yourself this question; Would I rather have an athlete that can run forever, but who has no kick or would I rather have an athlete that has to fight to stay in the front, but if he is there, he will outkick everyone at the end of the race? You want the athlete, right? Why? Because the athlete will win more "big" races than the aerobic one pace wonder will. It is easier to add aerobic onto an athlete than it is to add athleticism to aerobic athletes, at least in the short time we have them in high school. A college coach may see it the other way, as the races are longer and they may want the aerobic one pace wonder who may adapt better for the increased race distance. Often though, you see college coaches recruiting the faster miler over the endurance stud. Kicker's win races, and that is what they are recruiting.

I believe someone who knows they are a great athlete is more likely to go into the race with more confidence than someone who is fit but may not have the strength to go up or down hills fast or make a big finishing move. Your athletes will face some difficult courses during the season, make sure that you are building athletes that can handle whatever type of course is thrown at them, as well as any type of competitor.

Another huge reason to focus on building athletes is the other side of the distance coin, it will pay off in track. You know who wins races in track and field? Athletes do! I always tell my teams that in cross country we learn how to run, but in track we learn how to run fast. We spend the first 7 months of the school year building athletes, and when we hit the track it pays off big time. In our program, the goal is to have every athlete capable of running their fastest lap of the 1600 as their last lap. They have developed aerobically to a level where they can run the first 3 laps of the race and still be in it, while having the anaerobic strength to own the final lap and have a chance at the win. At the 2016 California State Track & Field Finals, Isaac Cortes ran the final lap of the 1600 in 55.82 to win in 4:04.62. It was 106+ degrees. He came back a short time later to win the 800 in 1:50.75 with a 54.97 second last lap in that race. Capping off the night, Cole Spencer made a huge move in the 3200, going from 7th to almost winning in 8:51.85, closing the final lap in 55.90! These two senior athletes had worked hard to not only be very strong aerobically, but to be athlete's that could stay in the race and run extremely fast the last lap. This is why you do HIITS, speed ladders, plyos, and all the strength pieces. When they need to run fast, you have them ready to do so!

Mental Training

We often use visualization to prepare our athletes mentally for the course, but there are many other ways you can prep your athletes to be mentally ready on race day. Mental preparation is often knowing that you have everything in hand, that the surprises that may happen on that day are well within the realm of what you have practiced and prepared for. Make sure your athletes are as strong mentally going into races as they are coming out of them.

Visualizations are a key part of training the mental part of our game. Utilize them to program your athletes for the key courses they need to prepare for. As your athletes learn to use visualizations to prepare for courses, they can practice this on their own at home. Another great way to do visualizations is by watching a course run through or race video, having your athletes visualize being in that race. They get to see in real time where they would be, what they would do, and how they would feel.

Another very important mental preparation for your athletes is course memorization and race plan prep. It is easy today to cover with your athletes all of the major courses they need to know, making sure they know what to expect on each one. Where are the hills? Where should they push? What side of the course should they be on and when? Not only should you develop a race plan for the major courses you race often (especially championship ones), but your athletes should have those concepts memorized and visualized before they get to them, working to perfect them throughout the years they are on your team.

Training toughness is not always easy to do, but it comes with a consistent pressure applied during practice time. You have to put your athletes in difficult situations in practice, ones they have to mentally power through, so that they can learn how to utilize this skill when it matters. A great way to do this is to say we are doing 5x1000m repeats. When everyone is done and spent, offer up another thousand to only the "mentally tough" athletes on your team. Many will answer the call so they aren't left behind, but what you will find is that they learn that they have a lot more in them than they think they do. Your job is to teach them they are tough, train them to be tough, and make sure when you are lining up at races that they believe they are tougher than any other athlete on the line.

You Have to Want it More Than Your Peers

Everyone dreams of standing at the top of the podium at the end of the season as the best team in the country. Only one team for each gender gets that opportunity each year. You have to want it more than your peers! I often tell my athletes that I will make plenty of mistakes as their coach, but that the reality is I just need to consistently make fewer than my peers for us to be successful. On a scale of 1-10, how bad do you want it? I know lots of coaches that are under 5's on that scale, and it shows in their results. If you truly want to be successful, YOU have to make the right decisions, starting with where you coach. If you coach at a school that gives you 3 frosh athletes a year, you most likely aren't winning Nike Cross Nationals. The math shows that. So, if you are a 10, are you at the right place, at the right time, with the right motivation, to be able to show how good you actually are?

The first area to look at is time. How much time are you putting in each day? You can't say you are a 10 on the scale above, but only putting in 2-3 hours a day. It doesn't work that way. To be the best, you have to want it more. That means each day you put in as much time as it takes. If you are up until 2 am, because that is what it takes, then you are up until 2. The best knows this. They don't even ponder it, because you do what needs to be done, that is how you get ahead. I challenge you to spend more time as a coach this season than you did the last. Read more books, watch more videos, reach out to more coaching mentors, make your practices more complex by adding in more components. Spend the time that it takes to get better, and see if your team improves. If it does, challenge yourself to spend even more time.

Another key area is passion. Is your passion like a fire, or does it wane with the change of seasons? Passion is important, because when you are passionate about something, it will be in the forefront of your thoughts, and of your life. If it you aren't that passionate about something, then it will always take a backseat. Look at your life, what comes before coaching? Your spouse, kids, church responsibilities, teaching? Where does coaching fit in your life? If the truth is that it is last place to all of those other responsibilities, you have already answered the passion question. To be one of the elite coaches in the country, coaching has to be a lifestyle, a passion that burns inside you. It has to push you to do the work, regardless of the other things pulling at you at the time. I'm not saying that you shouldn't be a good parent, or help out at the church. What I'm saying is that you have to build your life AROUND coaching, not add coaching to an already busy life. An example in my life would be that nobody at church would expect to see me at Saturday events. They all know who I am, and they know where I'm going to be. They all know I'm Coach Soles, and that I will always give 100% to being the best coach for my athletes that I can. I still attend church, pay my tithing, and pray with my kids, but everyone in my life knows that I will meet my coaching responsibilities first. When those are completed, then I am available. As I've stated earlier in this book, it helps to marry well.

Extremely passionate coaches have a very high level of attention to detail. They know when and where they are supposed to be, and who they are supposed to be there with. Not only do I have a very detailed digital calendar that I use to map out where I am supposed to be, but I also keep a very detailed To Do List. If something ends up on my TDL, it gets done. I'm detailed like that, I can't remember everything, so I keep a record of what needs to get done so that I can ensure that it does. Be organized, be prepared, and focus on making sure everything that needs to get done, gets completed at the highest level possible. If you note that you didn't do something well, add to your TDL things that will help you improve on it. Be the most detailed coach you know.

The final concept is the will to win. Coaches that have a very high level will to win, don't say things like "you are all winners just for finishing." It isn't because that isn't true to some extent, it is because winning coaches are focused on producing winners. They are focused on imparting their will on those around them at such a high level that those they interact with will have to step it up just to keep up. Infect everyone you work around with the will to win, and do everything you can to bring them up to your level. This doesn't always make you popular, and can be very frustrating for some parents, assistants, and athletes. If you want to build a consistently winning program, you have to want it more than everyone else does, and you have to not be ashamed of it. Inject your will to win in everything that you do, from the warm-up, to team meetings, to race reflection. You are always looking at ways to try something new, for ways to get better. Want it more than your peers, or be prepared to shake their hand and tell them good race when they beat you.

Staying Focused on the End Goal and Peaking for Championship Season

Cross country seasons are long. Between illnesses, injuries, lack of focus, vacations, and drama, there are lots of things to keep your team from accomplishing the end goal it set out to do at the beginning of the season. The first thing to remember is that many of the components of a successful peak are practiced or figured out during the regular season. Use the big meets early on to identify any issues your athletes are having and correct them. If you notice your athletes took their warm-ups off too soon and stood their freezing cold waiting for the race to start, then that is chance to fix that for the future. Take note of all the little things and subtly over the season show your athletes how to do it correctly.

Teams that peak well aren't doing anything magical, they are just way more prepared than your team is. There are always teams like that in every state. No matter what, you get their best race, and their athletes are always like Terminators on the course. Why? They have a good coach and that coach has spent a lot of time working to make sure that those athletes are ready for what is going to happen. Consistent coaches peak their athletes well. They often can't even tell you how, because the trick is the consistency, not some magic potion at the end of the season.

On our team we enter a 9 week window where we focus on eating healthy, getting enough sleep, cutting out junk food and wasted calories, and making sure things like our Ferritin are perfect. During this time, everything takes a back seat to being prepared for the championship season. Define a time and set of rules for your kids to have them dialed when it matters the most.

Peaking is a term many use for being sharp and ready at the right time. A lot of coaches hate the term, and many manipulate it. I have seen countless coaches purposefully tank their team's chances of success in the early season. Why? So, when they are fresh and ready at the end of the season, the coach looks better. It is a slight of hand, the athletes haven't improved much, they just look faster because their coach has allowed them to. The reality of peaking for your team should be that they are mentally and physically at their maximum ability when it matters. They have been prepped and ready for all the scenarios that may happen, and they are driven to accomplish their goals, not scared or happy that they made it to a big meet. Here are the steps to peak your athletes for their championship meets:

1. build your mileage over the season, not cutting much until a week or two before your end goal race.

2. Don't cut too much, stay as normal as possible.

3. Run normal workouts on Monday, Tuesday, and Wednesday, and then go lighter on Thursday and Friday for a Saturday Meet. This keeps your body at its fitness level. Cutting back too much will

throw off your conditioning and your kids will feel flat.

4. Have your athletes mental prep dialed in over the entire season. They have to be just as mentally prepared as they do physically.

5. Have their race day prep down to a science. They know everything that works for them from what they should eat, drink, or listen to music wise, and they can execute everything they need to do without thinking about it. Make it a natural part of their race day. Do not coddle or assist them throughout the season, you don't want them relying on you, you want them prepared to do it all themselves on championship race day. If you can't be there, it won't matter, they are ready!

6. When you send them out to race, remind them of how prepared they are, and how much you care about them. I always tell my kids we will care about them just as much if they lose as if they win. Let them know you are there for them, and will support them no matter the outcome.

CHAPTER TWELVE: FINAL THOUGHTS

Cross country is one of the most pure and unique sports out there. The basicness of it makes it easy to learn, but the intricacies of it make it extremely hard to master. There are realistically very few coaches that are consistently competing for the national title each season, 3 to 6? Mastering this sport requires you to not only have a knack for it, but also enough passion to put in the time it requires to be successful long term. I've mentored lots of coaches who have started out doing great, but when it got tough or they hit a plateau they moved on to something else. It is the people that keep pushing, keep digging for one more good athlete, one more new workout, one more change in their seasonal rhythm that end up moving up the coaching depth chart. Greatness in cross country coaching is being able to set a goal, fail at accomplishing it, and getting back on the horse to try again without losing the faith and fervor that started you on the journey to begin with.

The most important thing that I have learned as a cross country coach is that consistency is the key to long term success. No matter what you do, if your athletes are not consistent, your results will show it and you will not be able to year in and year out compete for championship titles. The best way to stay consistent is to have a yearlong training concept, and a group of athletes that have bought into the fact that it is a yearlong development cycle to be truly good at this sport. Too many coaches treat each season as an individual piece of the pie, instead of looking at each year as an opportunity to grow tremendously aerobically. The athletes that struggle to improve the most are the ones that are the most inconsistent.

Keeping healthy is one of the biggest keys to consistency. Put in place a culture and a training program that is focused on developing athletes year over year, with consistency as the centerpiece. Consistency in running, eating, sleeping, core and strength development, visualizing, and competing. Those are the athletes that you want to build. Don't rush it! Plan it and execute it. Be patient and take your time. Give athletes the time they need to become great!

Greatness Isn't Free

To get to the top you will pay a heavy price. You need to go into any search for greatness understanding that, and be willing to pay that price to stay at the top. Greatness is missing your kid's soccer game. Greatness is seeing your spouse for 2-3 hours a day. Greatness is failing over and over again, and waking up with the same eagerness to go after success again. Greatness is exhaustion to the point that you can't possibly carry on, then pushing through and doing it anyway. Greatness takes a toll, and you need to know that before you start searching for it.

Many coaches don't want to be criticized by their peers, their athlete's parents, or their administration. The truth is that criticism is often a sign post that you are on the right path. When you are doing things that make others around you uncomfortable, you are challenging the status quo, and that gives you a chance to be great. Doing the basics never won anyone a championship. If everyone believes 40 miles a week is the right thing to do and everyone is doing that, then you will get results just like everyone else. You have to think outside the box and find *what gives your program the advantage*! Once you start winning, expect the critics to come out of the woodwork.

Their mileage is too high, they recruit, they kill those kids with really hard workouts, they are a private school, the coach cares too much, the coach cares too little about the kids, the school is bigger than most, the coach won't let the athletes take hard classes, the coach only cares about winning, the coach is taking away their college years by running them too hard, and on and on and on they will go. What this tells you is that the average people around you, the people who aren't willing to make the commitment that you are willing to make, are uncomfortable with what you are doing. You have left the status quo and are now on your own level. The trolls are uncomfortable with this and will say anything to make you look bad. Good, that means you are going the right direction. Don't listen to them, but hear that they are there, because they are there for a reason. They are there to show you that you are leaving the heard.

Greatness is almost by definition being ahead of the game. Your starting point is ahead of where everyone else is starting. As a cross country coach, greatness always meant that we were progressing ahead of where everyone else was at, that meets would be everyone vs. Great Oak. To get ahead of everyone else, you have to put in the time. I don't mean hanging out with the funny coach we all know, that is good at a few things but doesn't really put the work in to get to the next level. They are just happy to be out there, to have a place to belong. I'm talking about the guy that is putting in entries until 1:00 am and getting up at 5 to finish work. I'm talking about the coach that is working when everyone else is asleep. Running the numbers, identifying athletes they need, making phone calls, convincing that 400m girl to join cross in the fall, setting up a new fundraiser. The coaches that never stop working toward the end goal, and the end goal is so far out there that they don't really even know where it is. What is success to someone who isn't ever truly satisfied? Greatness is a price you choose to pay every single day. Not because you want to see your name in lights, but because you want to see your athlete's name in lights. You want to do everything you can to ensure they are prepared for the biggest stage. That's on you.

Thoughts and Quotes from Coach Soles' Twitter

I have often shared my thoughts about coaching on Twitter and wanted to add some of those thoughts here with a breakdown of my thinking when I tweeted them. Don't be afraid to voice your opinions or ideas as a coach, but realize not everyone will get you. The power of words isn't in what you say, but in how others interpret it.

Coach Soles Tweets

"If we listen to people without the knowledge, we will suffer the consequences of their ignorance." This quote was a reminder to the athletes on my team to know who to listen to. Often athletes will listen to other teens who are just guessing at accurate information and it ends up a bad version of telephone, or their parents who have never run before. It is a reminder to seek out the source of information and to listen to credible sources, not rumors or opinions.

"You have a champion's mindset. Most coaches do not. Most just want to be a part of the process, relive their glory days, but they don't want to actually compete at a level that creates expectations on them. Most don't want the stress winning creates." I am responding to a coach in this quote, really trying to differentiate between coaches that go after it, and coaches that just want to be a part of the sport. Which one are you?

"At the end of the day, if you let a vampire into your life, don't be surprised when your payment is in blood. Own your risks, own your decisions." This was a reminder to me that if I let my ego get too big, that I will pay the price for it. I was debating running our "B" team at CIF Finals, and this was a reminder to myself that I needed to own that risk, not anyone else.

"Every day our athletes are auditioning for our top 7 in XC. I'm always amazed at how many take themselves out of the running, simply by seeing opportunity as work." This quote was something I shared after seeing a couple boys on my team with the talent to be top 7 guys, who just really didn't want to do the work. They had every opportunity to be one of the best on our team, but they didn't want all the responsibility that came with. They were content to go through the motions, and I was reminding them that we as coaches can see that.

"One of the biggest mistakes I see coaches make is letting other people (Admin, Parents, Naysayers, etc.) have a say in their vision. Your job is to make that vision happen, and to get around every obstacle those who lack vision or solutions put in your way. Find a way!" This was me trying to remind cross country coaches to run the show! Have a vision and eliminate the people in your coaching world that don't want to get on board with it!

"The dumbest successful coach I ever met once said to me "Let them fire me! I was looking for a job when I found this one." This was a coach I spoke with when I was a young coach. He was successful, his athletes loved him, but he saw the solution to most adversity as quitting or getting fired. He should have been looking for ways to communicate and build trust, instead he was always on the move because he couldn't work well with others.

"He had no fear and consequently had no issue implementing his vision. Fear is very powerful, but is also something we can talk ourselves out of." This goes along with the previous quote. He was successful because he had no fear of being fired. He had mastered fear, because he was going to coach his way and if he lost his job he would simply move on. Awesome to watch, but also sad to see someone with a lot of potential never reach their potential because they had already decided outcomes before they were put in them. His was going to quit or get fired, and as far as he was concerned, it was someone else's fault.

"Coaches, be careful getting caught up with what Freak A or Freak B are doing for workouts. Their coaches could give them 3 miles a day they would still win. Focus on developing workouts that develop your 5-10 on your team. If you make them better, then you're coaching!" I look at social media often, and when you do that you see so many amazingly talented athletes each season. The truth is though, many of those athletes are successful because they have freak level talent. They are going to be good in any program in America. The coaches you want to learn from are the ones that can teach you how to develop talent, not just exploit the talent they find.

How to Win NXN

As a high school coach there is no higher level of team success than standing at the top of the Nike Cross Nationals podium. In many cases, years have gone in to building and tweaking a team to be ready to compete against the best in the nation. The hard thing about cross country is not only do you have to face the best the nation, you have to face them all at once. No other sport pits every team against every other team at the same time the way cross country does. One bad race by one of your top athletes and your hopes and dreams of winning the big one is immediately over. How you build your team is critical for winning NXN.

Be prepared for All-star teams and Superteams to form and understand that when you take on everyone in the country, there will always be one of these to face. Some years you get a team that has 2, 3, or 4 big transfers and all of a sudden, they are the top ranked team in the nation. The way things look at the end of a track season can change a lot over the summer as some athletes improve, some mature, and transfers occur. The truth is, it is very hard to win NXN without a transfer or an unfair advantage like being able to use middle schoolers. If you pull it off, you've developed one heck of a crew along the way!

Winning NXN requires the building of a roster that can mathematically have a chance at not only qualifying, but scoring few enough points that you are in contention. Any weakness you have will instantly be magnified and exploited at a meet of this caliber. The majority of the teams won their state titles and know what it takes to compete with the best. The rosters below have a great chance of winning NXN:

- **3 Superstars Team** – In 2015, our boys team had 3 guys that were all good enough to be number one on the team and top 25 at NXN. Anyone of those 3 guys could have run for an individual state title on a good day, so we felt like we had 3 number ones that fall. Behind them we had Solomon Fountain, who went on to run 4:10 for the 1600 as a junior that spring. Tony

Robinson who had struggled with injuries throughout his career but had the ego and intelligence that we felt would pay off on a tougher course like NXN. Nelson Quintana who was more of a middle distance guy, but someone who had paid off for us many times before when we needed him most. Nelson ran 1:50 for the 800 and had a top 5 finish at New Balance Nationals later that spring. Brandon Shields was our 7th guy coming into the meet, he was our hard worker. He was the guy that killed it over the summer to move into contention for the top 7. We finished with 3 guys in the top 27, and 2 more guys in the 80's. We won by 49 points. These teams are only as good as the ability of #4 and #5 to finish inside the top 100 or so. 3 superstars with no depth behind it will lose every time. Develop that depth and you have a very good chance of winning! Never underestimate the actual talent it takes to win this event!

- **Tight Pack Team** – In 2019, our boys team had a tight pack all season. We finished with a 10 second spread at NXN and ended up losing the meet by 4 points to a very talented Newbury Park team who used the 3 superstar approach. To get very tight packs, **_all 7_** of your athletes need to be on the same ability plane, meaning most of the time at least 5 of them will finish within a small gap from each other. These teams typically have no national front runner, but everyone on the team is very good and can run between 40-70th place at NXN before individuals are taken out. These teams often have a great chance at winning and are easier to build than teams that require superstars. It is harder to find a superstar than it is to build a very good runner.

- **No Weaknesses Team** – This team may not have a super close team spread or a specific number of superstars, but rely more on the fact that they have no real weaknesses. Their number 4 and number 5 will finish high enough in the results that they may be able to win (top 60 overall). These teams have a high probability of winning NXN, usually under 100 point scores. Loudoun Valley's boys' teams are a great example of teams that had very few weaknesses and were able to dominate at NXN.

- **All-Star Team** – Unfortunately, this team seems to be all too common lately. It is a team filled with athletes that either started at another high school, or were supposed to go to another high school. Usually, super deep and talented because their athletes are a collection of talent from all over. These teams win, but are not traditional high school teams and need more of a manager, than a coach. Give any coach in the country 7 guys who can run 9:00 flat for 3200, and almost all of those coaches will win the NXN title with that group.

Since I began coaching, I have always heard that rankings don't matter. The National Rankings matter! They matter because they show you who you need to prepare for and what type of team they are. Where did they start in the rankings? Where are they now? Why did they move up? This list is compiled to show you who to prepare for and how to prepare your race strategy. Some years it might be you versus one specific team, and you may know them well. Other years it may be teams that come on late in the year from a state that doesn't get a lot of coverage. In 2019, we knew that Corner Canyon (UT) would be a good team, but they didn't run a lot of top invitationals and we had limited data on them (state meet). National rankings give you an idea of how your team is perceived, how the other teams are perceived, what everyone's perceived strengths and weaknesses are, and what you need to do to plan for all scenarios. Rankings are just opinions, but they are full of information. Don't ignore the data that is being given to you for free!

Portland Meadows was not a cross country course. It was a swamp. There was no reason to have a championship meet there to determine who had the best team in the nation. Teams that were running Tough Mudder competitions would have been much more prepared for that course than a normal cross country team from any part of the nation. The problem became that the course itself was an entity, and had a major role to play in the outcome at the meet. Just like in other sports, you don't want the ref to determine the winner, you want the ability of the teams to be the overall reason they win or lose. Things had to change.

Fortunately for all of us in 2014, Nike Cross Nationals moved to Glendoveer Golf Course in Southeast Portland and a lot of the nightmares that happened at Portland Meadows were lessened. Lots be honest, it is Portland in December. It will be wet. It will be cold. There will be mud. The move to the new course negated a lot of the impact that these issues had on the overall outcome compared to Portland Meadows. These issues are still there and are still having an impact, but they do not dictate results like Portland Meadows did. The new course is more a course that everyone in the country will see at some point in their season.

What type of course strategy does it take to win Nike Cross Nationals? Obviously, there are many factors, including course conditions, how good your competition is that year, how deep your team is, and your teams' usual style of racing. On a super muddy course, your team may want to get out much faster than you usually do, as moving up through the field on tired legs and in the mud is very difficult. You will notice that in the muddy years, very little changes happen in places for your athletes past the first mile. In dryer years, it is possible to sit back a little more the first mile and start moving up past the athletes that have gone out too fast. No matter what, you have to calculate where your athletes should be moving to and make sure they are aware of the math. The last mile is typically the easiest part of the course, excluding the final two inclines. Have your athletes in position with a mile to go, and aerobically strong enough to compete when it matters.

As you evolve into a national class program, your circle of competition is no longer local. Every bit of cross country news around the country is something you have to watch, as it can change who you will be facing for the title that season or in the future. Club teams, frosh transfers, regular transfers, schools closing, schools opening, state rules changes, etc. all factor in what you will be dealing with on your path to the top. Be prepared for a rollercoaster ride!

How NXN Could Be Better

Props to Josh Rowe in 2004 getting Nike to start an event that gives us a chance to bring the best of our sport together to see who is the best of the best. There truly isn't a better opportunity for any team in the country to show that they are the best in the nation. Nike has done every cross country coach a tremendous service by supporting our sport like they do. When I first started at Great Oak, I was the only person on our team wearing Nike shoes. Now almost all of our coaches and athletes do. A major reason for this has been a grassroots effort by Nike to reach down to the youth to build the popularity of our sport. We all owe people like Josh Rowe a big thank you.

Having said that, we must understand that NXN is a marketing event that we use to determine a champion. I had the chance to ask Josh what the thinking was behind the start of the event and try to understand why the rules were set up the way they were. What I learned was they were just worried about getting the meet started. They weren't worried about balance, equal rules, or the results. They were creating a fun event for kids, and a marketing event for Nike. That was the depth of the thinking from what I can tell. Unfortunately, the rules are not the same for everyone and it is reflected in the results, especially on the girl's side. Some states are allowed to use middle school runners, while others are not. Many have tried to say this isn't an issue, but it is because it creates a tremendous imbalance between states that can use their younger runners, and the states that cannot. I've often said that my 2010 and 2011 girls' teams would have been tremendously better had I been able to use Destiny Collins as a middle schooler. She ran 9:53 for 3200 and 15:58 for 3 miles in cross country while at Great Oak. Can you imagine the mathematical advantage she would pose for our teams if we could run middle schoolers and nobody else could? I would have been able to tie her together with athletes she never knew and never ran with. She would have made everyone on the team better, similar to how Sarah Baxter made all the girls at Simi Valley better when she arrived as a frosh. No other championship would allow some teams to play by certain rules, and other teams to not. It makes no sense, unless you look at it through the lens of why Nike does it. It is a marketing tool. The results don't matter. This is a major reason why the girls race takes a back seat to the boys race each season. The coaches and athletes know the girls' race isn't being contested on an even playing ground. Can you imagine yourself sitting down to play poker and you get your two cards in Texas Hold'em, only to see your opponent's getting three? How long would you stay at that table with those odds? Would you play basketball against a team that was allowed 6 players to your five? Professional blackjack players often negotiate the rules with the house before they sit down to bet millions of dollars to give themselves the best chance to win. Would you sit and play blackjack knowing the rules were heavily skewed in the houses favor, or would you negotiate? The biggest problem that we run into is that this problem only really effects a few coaches. Most coaches of girls' teams that make it are so happy to be at the event, that they aren't thinking about the rules, they just want to be a part of the game. Until Nike changes that concept, the girls' race will always be second tier at NXN and the results will continue to be skewed in favor of the teams allowed this advantage. Every team at NXN should be competing under the exact same rules, currently that is not the case. I hope that it is changed in the future to ensure everyone at the meet is competing under the same rules.

I personally would prefer to see NXN as a rotating course of 4-6 different courses across the nation that fit the requirements for a championship meet. This would allow for all coaches having to continuingly make adjustments for weather, different course conditions, travel time, humidity, and would break up the rhythm advantage that teams have that make the meet year in and year out and master how to be prepared in Portland. Put on meets in Portland, California, Texas, Florida, North Carolina, New York for example. I believe rotating to various regions would make the meet change in a way that would prevent consistent benefits for any specific region, and allow for different parts of the country to highlight the event. No specific region would have a regular course advantage, and the coaches would be forced to adapt to new courses consistently. This won't happen because it is a marketing event and not a regulated championship, but it would be awesome to see this as a change in the future.

What is the Secret?

Every program has the little things they do that put them over the top. Here are some final thought secrets from our program that have allowed us to consistently compete with the best teams in the nation each season.

If you truly want to build a cross country dynasty, you need to develop a **year-round focus**, and not just focus on the current season. You need to use every day in that year to make your athletes better! A 19:00 frosh girl, should be an 18:00 soph girl, and an 17:30 or better junior girl, and a 17:00 senior girl or better as they develop. Obviously, it doesn't always work that way, but the more athletes you develop like this the more weapons you will have to choose from when it comes time to compete for state titles! Athletes that take seasons off give back many of the gains they gained during the cross country season. If they go play something like basketball in the winter then you will get them back in a similar place for track that you got them at the start of the cross country season. They won't be improving season over season, and instead you will just be trying to get out of them what their talent allows them to be in any individual season instead of what they could be with consistent season over season development. Summer is your cross-country base, fall is your cross country season, winter is indoor track or spring track base building, and spring track completes the year. Athletes that take a couple weeks after fall and spring season will be ready to come back and develop more aerobically dominant and ready for faster paces the following year. They won't be starting over. Build a yearlong plan and get your athletes to buy into it!

One of the biggest keys to athletic development is **year round HIIT training** (running and core based). HIIT's build athletes up to be able to handle the rigors the mile or hills place on the body. They teach athletes how to make or handle moves made in a race. They are easy to implement, take very little time in your training plan, and help burn fat that consistent aerobic training might not burn. The big key with them is building them up over time and making sure your athletes are strong enough to handle the rigors of the paces.

If you want to be successful as a coach, you need to keep your athletes as healthy as possible. Setting aside time for **consistent core** and form work to focus on strength and efficiency, increase your athlete's injury prevention ability, their athleticism, their ability to handle other workloads, and overall fitness. Often core is an afterthought. In our program we block off 30 minutes of time after our warm-up to ensure we do it well each day.

Teach **competition in practice**. Your job is to create athletes that are used to and prepared for the battles they will face on the course. Some athletes are natural born predators, they will attack anything that moves in a competition, but many must learn how to be competitive. Develop a list of 5 or more activities that you do in your program that actively encourages competition between your athletes and incorporate them regularly, especially during the base phase when competition is limited. It can be as simple as racing up the stairs in a stadium routine, but they must practice winning and losing, and how to handle both.

Teach **race strategies** for your athletes, so that they can read the situation in a race and understand not only what they are trying to do, but what their opponent might be trying to do to them. (sit & kick, go out hard and build big lead, big early move, push middle of race or certain point in race, etc.). Athletes that are educated on what moves they can make, and what moves may be made on them will instinctively be more prepared to respond correctly and adequately when those situations arise. It is your responsibility to educate them, put them in these situations, and try these different moves with your athletes so they are as prepared as they can be on race day.

Focus on developing **athleticism** in your athletes so that they have finishing speed in cross country and can run the last 400m of a race faster than their opponents (last rep fastest one in repeat workouts). The aerobic component of distance running is obvious, and if someone just focused all of their attention on that one detail, their team could do some pretty good things. The truth today though, is that more and more of the top runners aren't aerobic monsters, they are tremendous athletes. They are capable of running up and down hills at tremendous speeds! They are capable of incredible finishes! They are putting on tremendous moves in the middle of races to break their competition! Your athletes have to have the physical strength and agility to handle everything thrown at them on any style of course. Focus on building their athleticism so that they are ready for the challenges they will face, not just their aerobic engine.

Our program spends a lot of time on **extra core**, doing things like med balls, plyo boxes, and core HIIT's. All of these items are in addition to the regular core routines we do every single day to make sure we are fit. Why? One of the main reasons is physical strength. We want our athletes as strong as they can be, without adding any additional weight that may slow them down on the course. Using 10-15 minutes at the end of practice to further develop the strength and core of our athletes is critical in making sure they can handle a 6 month season and many of the biggest races in the country.

One area I fought for a long time in our program was doing **hills and stadium routines.** My main reason was they were so short in duration, and so intense on the athlete's body, that I didn't' feel we would get enough out of them. It turns out that adding these simple workout components to our program once a week each, really increased the physical strength of our athletes, and allowed us to not only physically handle courses like Mt. SAC, but also to mentally prepare for the feeling of going up and down steep hills. Take the time to add these components into your training plan for a cheap and easy boost to your athlete's overall strength and athleticism on the course.

Build **distance athletes**, not distance runners! The truth is that aerobic monsters or one pace wonders always win until they match up with someone that has just enough juice to stay close to them, and then they get outkicked. This usually happens when it matters the most, at the state or national meet. There is almost always someone out there that can stay with you, even if they don't know they can. You want to be aerobically very strong as a cross country runner, but you also want to be athletic enough to handle hills, starts, finishes, moves made by other runners, and other obstacles the course will throw at you.

Being a Good Teammate

We had one season where the athletes really struggled to get along with each other. We sat down with the girls' team, and reached out to some of our alumni about what being a good teammate meant to them. This list was formed <u>by the girls</u> and the coaches, and does a great job of outlining what is important in being a good teammate.

- Encourage each other.
- Support each other, especially the younger kids.
- Be happy for each other.
- Push each other to be your best.
- Put the team first before personal goals.
- No talking behind your teammates back.
- Run for each other.
- Trust your coaches!
- It's not about you.
- Know what and who you are running for.
- Communicate.
- Be honest.
- Respect each other's uniqueness, and don't be jealous of each other.
- Understand that you will have competition from your teammates, but your real competition is the other team.
- Work together.
- Know how to compromise.
- Do the workout given by the coaches.
- Be willing to sacrifice for your teammates.
- Set aside your differences at practice.
- Take ownership of your actions.
- Hold each other accountable.
- Live the Golden Rule.
- Live by a positive quote or mantra.
- PMA – Positive Mental Attitude.
- Build each other up.
- Plan your successes together.
- Love your teammates.
- Desire success for your teammates.
- Be there for your teammates.
- Celebrate when they are happy and comfort the when they are not.
- Tolerate no gossip, malice, or exclusion.
- Be a leader to your teammates.
- Speak when needed, or set an example.
- Be a follower of your teammates and listen.
- Work hard.
- Maintain an attitude/mentality which are positive, uplifting, committed, tenacious, and mature – for your sake

and your teammates'.
- Know how to graciously accept success and defeat (which is only temporary).
- Be a normal human being! Find a balance in life... as great and important as running is, if it's all you have, you'll never recover from adversity.

For Your Athletes – The Essential Top 10 Don't Do's in Running

Don't:

1. Get your wisdom teeth pulled during the season or preseason training period. It can take 2-6 weeks to return to where you were before the surgery. Plan this during the beginning of your 2-week break after either cross country or after spring track.

2. Give blood during the season or preseason training. It can take you two or more weeks to return to where you were before you gave blood!

3. Take Accutane or any other acne medication without first informing your coach you are on it. It really affects your running and will cause you to fall way behind in training and races. There are oftentimes other medications that won't affect you endurance wise, see if you can try one of those first. Always communicate with your coach what actions are being taken, as some will keep you from being able to run at your best.

4. Take an extended vacation in the middle of the summer training or season. Planning ahead and doing your vacation early in the summer and during your break from running or as you start back up training can help save your season!

5. Take coaching advice from <u>ANYONE</u> other than your coach! All this does is confuse you, and potentially keeps you from improving. Always listen to your coaches, and let others know that you get training and racing advice from your coaches only.

6. Ignore taking iron supplements until your Ferritin (iron stores) gets low and THEN try to figure out why you are running slowly. A good Ferritin score for a high level runner is between 80-100. If you are under 30 you will run much slower. Taking iron supplements should happen daily. Get your Ferritin checked once each of the 3 seasons. Work with your parents to schedule your supplements. Coming back from athletic induced anemia can take months!

7. Schedule your PSAT, SAT, or ACT tests on days we have meets. Plan ahead, schedule them during summer or winter where you will not need to miss being there for your team! We support you academically, but your teammates need you at the meet. Proper planning will help you not miss any meets.

8. Join a bunch of clubs or other outside activities that take you away from your running. If you want to be successful at running long term, you must eliminate outside conflicts like club sports, clubs at school, etc. Remember that there are only so many hours in the day. Focus on academics, running, and having a social life.

9. Leave your phone on when you go to bed! Make sure to turn it off so you won't be awakened by a call or text at 2 in the morning by someone who doesn't sleep! Rest is your best friend and your best way to stay healthy! Unplug every night by 9:00 pm and you will sleep much better.

10. Skip a season of running and expect to be a varsity athlete. There are 4 training seasons: Summer XC, Fall XC, Winter Track, Spring Track. You will not progress as a runner long term if you are taking months off at a time. You essentially will start over when you return to training the next season and all your hard work will be lost.

CONCLUSION

Building Championship Cross Country Programs is not easy. Ultimately, **you** are the key to the success of your program. The amount of time you choose to spend preparing, building, improving, and defining the success of your program will determine the overall results each season. To be the best, you have to consistently believe that you are working to be the best. You have to consistently try to find your weaknesses and fix them. We were able to turn Great Oak into one of the best programs in history because we never stopped working at it. Every season was an opportunity to change, adjust, modify, and try again at improving our team.

Ultimately, find the rhythm to your season! Find a way to create a seasonal roadmap that you know, understand, and can continue to improve year over year. Remember that competition matters, consistency matters, and challenging everyone around you to be at their best is critical to continue to improve. Work with your athletes to set the goals that inspire them to be great, and lead by example. Outwork everyone and leave no doubt in your mind that you have done everything that you can to be the best coach of your program.

Remember, no matter what this is your team. **Run the SHOW**!

AFTERWORD

Where is Coach Soles Now?

The one guarantee in coaching, is that nothing lasts forever. Wins, losses, dynasties, schools, jobs, none of it will last forever. At some point we move on, we reflect, we find the next phase. For me, the next step in that journey was a move with my family to Utah. I was able to find a job that was a great fit for what I wanted to build in the next phase of my coaching. Herriman High School in Utah was a school that had talent, but lacked competitive direction. In my first season as the head cross country coach (2022), our boys won the most competitive invite in Utah at Timpanogos, the biggest invite in the country in Woodbridge Cross Country Classic (CA), and finished 3rd place at NXN, making the podium for the 7th time in my coaching career. If you are doing the right things, the success will follow you wherever you go. Big things to come!

EPILOGUE
Appendix: Warm-ups, HIITS, and Workouts

Below are documents to help coaches create their training plan and have been used successfully by Coach Soles over many years.

XC Practice Warm-up

Warm-Up – 15-25 minutes

1. 1200m: (Field)
o Lap 1 warm up pace
o Lap 2 stride the straight-aways
o Lap 3 accelerate pace – finish with 200 at LT pace

2. Leg and Hip Swings – 10 front – 10 side – 10 circles – 10 hurdles (each leg)

Each drill is 20 meters in length and finish with a 20 meter stride back to start

3. High knees

4. Butt Kickers

5. "A" Skips

6. "B" Skips

7. Toe "Russian" Skip

8. G drill (combine 3-7)

9. Lunges

10. Ankle Walks

11. Speed ladder drills*

12. Carioca (left and right)

13. 4x60m accelerations

14. HIIT (on HIIT days only)

XC Meet Warm-up

Adopted and modified over the years from Coach Ken Reeves.

Meet Warm-up for Cross Country Team
Warm-up as a group with your fellow race athletes and listen to your race leaders and coaches.

Prerace Routine (Begin 40 minutes before your race)
-3-10 minutes of
easy running
-Leg
Swings
-Drills (high knees, butt kickers, "A"
Skips & "B" Skips,)
-5 minute cutdown run beginning easy for a minute, then each minute is faster until at
3200 race
pace.
-Put on racing flats/
spikes
-4-6 strides at race pace (simulate race start for
first 20m) (60m strides)
-Stay loose and do not
sit down.

Warm-Down –
Routine
-After a race, put on warm-ups and warm-down with 10-20+ minutes of easy running.
-Stretch as needed.

Items of
Note:
-Do NOT take off your warm-ups until it you have to!
-Make sure to get in 3-4 more quality strides once you get to the line to stay warm for racing. -You never know how long it will take them to start a race, so don't just stand there!
-Always know the meet schedule for all meets.
-Keep an eye out for your teammates to see if they fell asleep or forgot the warm-up time.
-Keep moving at the starting line and keep your blood and muscles going!
-Take care of bathroom needs before you begin warm-up. Lines can be long, so plan ahead!
-Make sure that you have a meet food routine that works for you and stick with it. You have to have fuel in your body, but make sure it is the right kind!
-Keep hydrated by drinking your WATER & sports drinks (not all one or the other) during the day.
-Check and make sure you have racing shoes and that they are in working order.
-Watch & support all races you are not running in. It is important to learn from others mistakes or great moves by watching others race.
-Have a positive race saying that you say to yourself every time you are called to the line!
-Do you need a bib number? Who is getting your warm-ups for you?
-The only real goal is to get to the line ready to compete!
-Be ready to run for your **teammates**!

2019 Varsity Boys Training Schedule

2019 Great Oak XC Varsity Training Calendar
May - June

*Do 1-2 of the strength routines every day + 100 pushups and 300 sit-ups. Focus on strength this summer! Who are your training partners to help you improve?

2nd workouts -
-Get access to a stationary bike!
-Secure a pool to swim in this summer!
-Make sure to swim or aqua jog, not just splashing around!

No workout should ever be slower than 8:00 pace!

Sunday	Monday	Tuesday	Wednesday	Thursday	Friday	Saturday
Rest 12	Aerobic 13	Recovery 14	Fartlek 15	Recovery 16	Training Run 17	Aerobic 18
Rest or Bike/Swim MAY	Morn: 3 miles After: 4 miles	Morn: 3 miles After: 4 miles + CH1	Morn: 3 miles After: 2 min ON 3 min OFF Interval for 30 min	Morn: 3 miles After: 4 miles + CH2	Morn: 3 miles After: 4 miles faster pace	Long Run 7 miles + CH3
Recov 19	TR 20	Recovery 21	Fartlek 22	Recovery 23	TR 24	Aerobic 25
Rest or Bike/Swim	Morn: 3 miles After: 5 miles faster pace	Morn: 4 miles After: 6 miles + CH1	Morn: 3 miles 2 min ON 3 min OFF Interval for 35 min	Morn: 3 miles After: Swim, Aqua Jog, Bike for 30 min + CH2	Morn: 4 miles After: 5 miles TR	Long Run 8 miles + CH3
Recov 26	Aerobic 27	Recovery 28	Fartlek 29	Recovery 30	Hills 31	Aerobic 1
Rest or Bike/Swim JUNE	Morn: 3 miles After: 7 miles w/3 three min pushes	Morn: 5 miles After: Swimming + CH1	Morn: 3 min ON 2 min OFF Interval for 35 min After: 6 miles	Morn: 4 miles After: 6 miles + CH2	Morn: 6 miles + 5xhills After: 3 miles	Long Run 9 miles + CH3
Rest 2	TR 3	Tempo 4	Recovery 5	Fartlek 6	Hills 7	Aerobic 8
Rest or Bike/Swim (HIT 10 on 20 off for 1 min)	Morn: 6 mile TR After: HIT + 5 miles recovery	Morn: 2x2 mile tempos w/3 min rest + 4 mile cool down run After: Swimming or Aqua Jogging + CH1	Morn: 9 miles After: HIT + 5 miles	2 min ON 1 min OFF Interval 39 min Afternoon WO Aqua Jogging + CH2	Morn: 7 miles After: HIT + 5 miles + 5xhills	Long Run 10 miles After: Biking + CH3
Recov 9	TR 10	LT 11	Recov 12	Fartlek 13	Hills 14	Aerobic 15
Rest or Bike/Swim (HIT 10 on 20 off for 1 min)	Morn: 6 mile TR After: HIT + 6 miles	Morn: 3x12 min LT runs w/3 min rest + 3 mile cool down After: 4 miles + CH1	Morn: 10 miles After: HIT + 6 miles	Morn: 3 min ON 2 min OFF Interval 45 min After: Stationary bike or swim + CH2	Morn: 6 miles After: HIT + 5 miles + 5xhills	Long Run 11 miles After: Biking + CH3

TR = Boys Training Run Pace = 6:00-6:15 range
TR = Girls Training Run Pace = 7:00-7:15 range

2019 Great Oak XC Varsity Training Calendar
June - July

*Do not forget to do
Warm up drills before
your workout.
Make sure to do stretching &
ice baths after!

Want to get better? Try adding
in 200+ pushups & 400 crunches
+ 2 minutes of planks for a 2nd
core routine every day.

No workout should ever be slower than 8:00 pace!

Sunday		Monday		Tuesday		Wednesday		Thursday		Friday		Saturday	
Recov	16	LT	17	Recov	18	Fartlek	19	Recov	20	Tempo	21	Aerobic	22
Rest or Bike/Swim JUNE (HIT 15 on 15 off for 1 min)		2 x 5,5,5 @ 70%, 80%, 85%+ w 5 min rest in between + 3 miles After: HIT + 6 miles		Morn: 11 miles After: Swimming + CH1		Morn: 3 min ON 1 min OFF Interval 40 min After: HIT + 6 miles		Morn: 9 miles After: 7 miles + CH2		Morn: 4 mile tempo run (85%) + 2 mile cool down After: HIT + 6 miles		Long Run 12 miles After: Swimming + CH3	
Rest	23	LT	24	Recov	25	Fartlek	26	Recov	27	Tempo	28	Aerobic	29
Rest or Bike/Swim (HIT 15 on 15 off for 1 min)		Morn: 3x2 mile tempo runs w 3 min rest + 2 mile cool down After: HIT + 5 miles		Morn: 10 miles After: 5 miles + CH1		Morn: 4 min ON 2 min OFF Interval 44 min After: HIT + 4 miles		Morn: 10 miles After: 5 miles + CH2		Morn: 5 mile tempo run (85%) + 2 mile cool down After: HIT + 6 miles		Long Run 12 miles After: Biking + CH3	
Recov	30	LT	1	Aerobic	2	Fartlek	3	Aerobic	4	Tempo	5	Aerobic	6
Rest or Bike/Swim (HIT 20 on 10 off for 1 min) JULY		Morn: 2 x 7,7,7 @ 70%, 80%, 85%+ w 4 min rest in between + 3 miles After: HIT + 5 miles		Morn: 10 miles After: 5 miles + CH1		Morn: 4 min ON 2 min OFF Interval 48 min After: HIT + 5 miles		Morn: 10 miles After: 5 miles + CH2		Morn: 5 mile tempo run (85%) + 1 mile cool down After: HIT + 6 miles		Long Run 12 miles After: Swimming + CH3	
Recov	7	LT	8	Aerobic	9	Fartlek	10	Aerobic	11	Tempo	12	Aerobic	13
Rest or Bike/Swim (HIT 15 on 15 off for 1:30)		Morn: 3x2 mile tempo runs w 3 min rest + 2 mile cool down After: HIT + 4 miles		Morn: 10 miles After: 5 miles + CH1		Morn: 3 min ON 2 min OFF Interval 45 min After: HIT + 4 miles		Morn: 10 miles After: 5 miles + CH2		Morn: 8 miles w 3 two min pushes After: HIT + 6 miles		Long Run 13 miles After: Swimming + CH3	
Recov	14	RACE	15		16		17		18		19		20
Rest		Time Trial Afternoon Run 6 miles recovery		Regular Summer Practice								We leave for camp on 21st	

When you get to July 15th, you want to be ready to step on the line for the time trial knowing that you did everything you could to be prepared. The most important training of our year is during the summer! How you approach this on your own will truly determine your success this season! Consistency in your training plan (running everyday, doing doubles), along with doing a solid warm up, strength work & core, proper diet, taking iron, sleeping, and injury prevention (ice baths) can help you improve minutes from one season to the next. Work hard for your teammates! Who will you train with to push yourself to get better?

2019 Great Oak Varsity XC Training Calendar
July - August

Aerobic Running Pace:
*Boys – 6:40/mile
*Girls – 7:30/mile

Sunday		Monday		Tuesday		Wednesday		Thursday		Friday		Saturday	
Recov	14	Race	15	Aerobic	16	Tempo	17	Aerobic	18	Vo2	19	Aerobic	20
Rest		**First Day of Practice!**		Morning: 9 miles + CH1		Morning: HIT + 3-5 mile tempo + 1 mile		Morning: 8 miles + CH2		Morning: HIT + 4x1000mt + 3 miles + Plyos & Med Balls		11-13 miles + CH3	
		Time Trial (Var – 6 mile Eve recov run)		Afternoon: 6 miles		Afternoon: 4 miles		Afternoon: 7 miles		Afternoon: 6 miles			
TBD	21	TBD	22	TBD	23	TBD	24	TBD	25	TBD	26	TBD	27
*Leave for Mammoth Camp		C		A		M		P		WE		EK	
Rest	28	Tempo	29	Aerobic	30	Fartlek	31	Aerobic	1	Recovery	2	Race	3
Rest		Morning: HIT + 4 mile tempo + 2 miles + PMB		Morning: 10 miles + CH1		Morning: HIT + 30 min Fartlek 2 on, 1 off + 3 miles + PMB		Morning: 7 miles + CH2		Morning: HIT + 4 miles for racers – 6 miles for non racers		Baldwin Park 5K + 3 mile cool down or 12 miles + CH3	
		Afternoon: 7 miles		Afternoon: 6 miles		Afternoon: 7 miles		Afternoon: 7 miles		Afternoon: 4 miles or rest			
Rest	4	Tempo	5	Aerobic	6	Fartlek	7	Aerobic	8	Recovery	9	Aerobic	10
Rest		Morning: HIT + 4 mile tempo + 4x200 + PMB		Morning: 8 miles + CH1		Morning: HIT + 30 min Fartlek 2 on, 1 off + 3 miles + 100 PU, 200 SU, 20 star jumps		Morning: 7 miles + CH2		Morning: HIT + 8 miles + PMB		13 miles + CH3	
		Afternoon: 6 miles		Afternoon: 4 miles		Afternoon: 7 miles		Afternoon: 6 miles		Afternoon: 5 miles recovery			
Rest	11	Aerobic	12	Tempo	13	Aerobic	14	Vo2	15	Aerobic	16	Aerobic	17
Rest		Morning: 7 miles		Morning: 7 miles		Afternoon: HIT – 6 Miles + 100 PU, 200 SU, 20 star jumps		Morning: 4 miles		Morning: 7 miles		13 miles + CH3	
Switch to Aft practices		Afternoon: HIT + 7 miles + PMB + SV		Afternoon: 2x800&2m Tempo + 4x200 + CH1		**1st day of school**		Afternoon: 6x600 + 2 miles + CH2		Afternoon: HIT + 7 miles + PMB			
Rest	18	Aerobic	19	Tempo	20	Aerobic	21	Aerobic	22	Fartlek	23	Aerobic	24
Rest		Morning: 12 miles		Morning: 4 miles + 10 Stadiums (ES)		Morning: 7 miles		Morning: 4 miles + 10 Stadiums (EOS)		Morning: 7 miles		13 miles + CH3	
		Afternoon: HIT + 7x6ill Sprints +2m + PMB + SV		Afternoon: 4 mile tempo + 2 miles + CH1		Afternoon: HIT + 6 miles + NV		Afternoon: 7 miles + CH2		Afternoon: HIT + 30 min Fartlek - 2 on, 1 off + PMB 9th Time Trial 2			

2019 Great Oak Varsity XC Training Calendar
August - September

Aerobic Running Pace:
*Boys – 6:40/mile
*Girls – 7:30/mile

Sunday		Monday		Tuesday		Wednesday		Thursday		Friday		Saturday	
Rest	25	Hills	26	NXN WO	27	Aerobic	28	Aerobic	29	Pre-Race	30	Race	31
Rest		**Morning:** 12 miles **Afternoon:** HIT + 8xHill Sprints + 2 miles + PMB + SV		**Morning:** 4 miles + 10 Stadiums ES **Afternoon:** 4x1000 Sand Repeats + 5 miles + CH1		**Morning:** 7 miles **Afternoon:** HIT + 7 miles + 4x200 + NV		**Morning:** 4 miles + 10 Stadiums EOS **Afternoon:** 8 miles + CH2		**Morning:** 5 miles on the beach		Big Ditch - 3-4 miles	
Rest	1	Aerobic	2	Aerobic	3	Vo2	4	Aerobic	5	Race	6	Aerobic	7
Rest		Labor Day – HIT + 12 miles on your own		**Morning:** 5 miles **Afternoon:** HIT + 6 miles + SV		**Morning:** 7 miles **Afternoon:** 8x800 + 2 miles + CH1		**Morning:** 4 miles **Afternoon:** HIT + 4 miles or 7 miles		Cool Breeze Invite or 4 mile tempo + 2 miles + CH2		13 miles - CH3	
Rest	8	Hills	9	Tempo	10	Aerobic	11	NXN WO	12	Aerobic	13	Aerobic	14
Rest		**Morning:** 12 miles **Afternoon:** HIT + 9xHill Sprints + 2 miles + PMB + SV		**Morning:** 4 miles **Afternoon:** 3 mile tempo + 2 miles + CH1		**Morning:** 7 miles **Afternoon:** HIT + 7 miles + PMB + NV		**Morning:** 4 miles **Afternoon:** 5x800 Sand Repeats + 5 miles + CH2		No School **Morning:** 7 miles oyo **Afternoon:** HIT – 6 miles oyo		14 miles - CH3	
Rest	15	Hills	16	Prog Run	17	Recov	18	Fartlek	19	Pre-Race	20	Race	21
Rest		**Morning:** 12 miles **Afternoon:** HIT + 10xHill Sprints + PMB + SV		**Morning:** 5 miles **Afternoon:** 5 mile progression run + 1 mile + CH1		**Morning:** 7 miles **Afternoon:** HIT + 7 miles + 3x150 + PMB + NV		**Morning:** 4 miles **Afternoon:** 21 minute Fartlek – 2 on 1 off + 2 miles + CH2		**Morning:** 3 miles **Afternoon:** 2 miles Team Meetings		Woodbridge Invitational (*3 mile cooldown run*)	
Rest	22	Hills	23	Blend Int	24	Aerobic	25	Vo2	26	Aerobic	27	Race	28
Rest		**Morning:** 12 miles **Afternoon:** HIT + 10xHill Sprints + PMB + SV		**Morning:** 5 miles **Afternoon:** 3x2000@race pace, 2 min jog, 200m @ mile pace, 4 min jog between sets + CH1		**Morning:** 7 miles **Afternoon:** HIT + 7 miles + PMB + NV		**Morning:** 4 miles **Afternoon:** 8x600 + 3x150 + 2 miles + CH2		**Morning:** 7 miles **Afternoon:** HIT + 6 miles + 4x200 or 3 miles for DH athletes		Dana Hills Invite + 3 miles Or 14 miles + CH3	

215

2019 Great Oak Varsity XC Training Calendar
October

Aerobic Running Pace:
*Boys – 6:40/mile
*Girls – 7:30/mile

Sunday	Monday	Tuesday	Wednesday	Thursday	Friday	Saturday
Rest 29	Hills 30	NXN WO 1	Aerobic 2	Race 3	Tempo 4	Race 5
Rest	**Morning:** 13 miles **Afternoon:** HIT + 10xhill sprints + PMB + SV	**Morning:** 5 miles **Afternoon:** 4x800 Sand Intervals + 2x200 SI + 5 miles + CH1	**Morning:** 7 miles **Afternoon:** HIT + 7 miles + NV or 3 miles	**Morning:** 4 miles **Afternoon:** SWL #1 or HIT + 4 mile tempo + 3x150 + CH	**Morning:** 3 miles **Afternoon:** 3 miles + strides or Course Run Through	Great American or Temecula Twilight + 3 miles
Recov 6	Tempo 7	Aerobic 8	Blend Int 9	Aerobic 10	CRT 11	Race 12
Rest	**Morning:** 5 miles **Afternoon:** HIT + 3 mile tempo + 4x200 + PMB + SV	**Morning:** 5 miles **Afternoon:** 10 miles + CH1	**Morning:** 7 miles **Afternoon:** HIT + 3x2000@3200 race pace. 2 min jog. 300m @ 800 pace. 4 min jog btwn	**Morning:** 4 miles **Afternoon:** 7 miles + CH2 + NV	**Afternoon:** Course Run Through + 3-4 miles	Clovis Invite + 4 miles
Rest 13	Hills 14	Aerobic 15	Race 16	Tempo 17	NXN WO 18	Aerobic 19
Rest	**Morning:** 13 miles **Afternoon:** HIT + 10xhill sprints + PMB + SV	**Morning:** 5 miles **Afternoon:** 7 miles + 3x160m + CH1	**Morning:** 7 miles **Afternoon:** SWL #2 or HIT + 4 mile tempo + 3x150	**Morning:** 4 miles **Afternoon:** 6 miles + CH2 + NV	**Morning:** 7 miles **Afternoon:** HIT + 5x800 Sand Intervals - 2x200 SI + 5 miles	14 miles + CH3
Rest 20	Hills 21	Blend Int 22	Aerobic 23	Vo2 24	Aerobic 25	Race 26
Rest	**Morning:** 12 miles **Afternoon:** HIT + 10xhill sprints + PMB + SV	**Morning:** 5 miles **Afternoon:** 3x1600@3200 race pace. 2 min jog. 300m @ 800 pace. 4 min jog + 2 min rest between sets + 1 mile CD + CH1	**Morning:** 7 miles **Afternoon:** HIT + 7 miles	**Morning:** 4 miles **Afternoon:** 800, 600, 400, 600, 800 + 3x200 + 2 miles - CH2	**Morning:** 3 miles **Afternoon:** 2 miles + Pre Race Meetings	Mt. Sac Invitational + 5 mile Cooldown run
Rest 27	Sprints 28	Aerobic 29	Tempo 30	Aerobic 31	Race 1	Aerobic 2
Rest	**Morning:** 5 miles **Afternoon:** HIT + 4 miles + 6x200 + PMB	**Morning:** 5 miles **Afternoon:** 6 miles + CH1 + SV	**Morning:** 7 miles **Afternoon:** HIT + 3 mile tempo + 2x200 fast	**Morning:** 3-4 miles **Afternoon:** 3 miles for racers or 7 miles + CH2	**Morning:** 7 miles or Rest **Afternoon:** Arcadia Invite or HIT + 6x800 + 3x150m	13 miles + CH3

2019 Great Oak Varsity XC Training Calendar
November - December

Sunday	Monday	Tuesday	Wednesday	Thursday	Friday	Saturday
Rest 3	Sprints 4	Aerobic 5	Race 6	Aerobic 7	Aerobic 8	Blend Int 9
Rest	Morning: 7 miles. Afternoon: HIT + 6x200 sprints + 2 miles + SV	Morning: 2-5 miles. Afternoon: 3-7 Miles + 3x150 (CH1 for Non-Racers)	Morning: 7 miles or Rest. Afternoon: SWL Finals - 3 miles or HIT + 4 mile tempo + 2 mile CD	Morning: 4 miles. Afternoon: 7 miles + CH2	Morning: 4 miles. Afternoon: 10 miles + PMB	3x1200@3200 race pace, 2 min jog, 400m @ 600 pace. 2 min jog + 3 mi + CH3 + NV
Rest 10	Aerobic 11	Aerobic 12	Tempo 13	Aerobic 14	Race or SI 15	Aerobic 16
Rest	NO SCHOOL. 13+ miles oyn	Morning: 4 miles. Afternoon: 6 miles (with hills) + 3x200 + CH1 + SV	Morning: 7 miles. Afternoon: Racers - HIT + 4x600 - 3x150 + 3 miles. Non Racers - HIT + 3 mile tempo + 3x150 +2 miles	Morning: 2-4 miles. Afternoon: 6 miles + 3x150 + PMB - Prelims racers just WU	Morning: 4 miles. CIF SS Prelims @ Riverside - 3 miles + Afternoon: HIT + 3x800 +2x300 fast finish + 3 miles	13 miles + CH3
Rest 17	Aerobic 18	Blend Int 19	Aerobic 20	Vo2 21	Aerobic 22	Race 23
Rest	Morning: 11 miles. Afternoon: HIT + 6xhill sprints + PMB + SV	Morning: 5 miles. Afternoon: 3x800@1600 race pace, 2 min jog, 400m @ 400 pace. 4 min jog + 2 min rest + 2 mi + CH1	Morning: 4-7 miles. Afternoon: HIT + 6 miles + 3x150 + PMB	Morning: 4 miles. Afternoon: 800-600-400-200-200 (120-90-60 sec rest) + 2 miles or 3 mile tempo + 3x150 + CH2	Morning: 2-4 miles. Afternoon: HIT + 6 miles + 3x200 or Finals athletes just WU	CIF SS Finals @ Riverside + 3 mile cooldown run or 3x400 @ goal 3200 pace 75 sec rest + 4x200 + 3 miles + CH3
Rest 24	Vo2 25	Aerobic 26	Tempo 27	Aerobic 28	Pre-Meet 29	Race 30
Rest	Morning: HIT + 5x600 + 4x200 + 3 miles + SV. Afternoon: 7 miles	Morning: 5 miles + 3x150 + CH1. Afternoon: 6 miles	Morning: HIT + 4 miles with 4 90 second pushes + 3x150. Afternoon: 5 miles	3 miles + 3x200m. Eat light at Thanksgiving Dinner	Morning: Travel to Fresno. Afternoon: Course Run Through (3 miles + Strides)	CIF State Championships @ Woodward Park - Fresno + 2 miles
Rest 1	Aerobic 2	Vo2 3	Aerobic 4	Pre-Meet 5	Pre-Meet 6	Race 7
Rest December	Morning: 10 miles. Afternoon: HIT + 1 mile + 5x200, Maint PMB + NV	Morning: 5 miles. Afternoon: 4x600 + 3x200 Sprints + 4 miles + CH1 + NV	Morning: 5 miles. Afternoon: HIT + 7 miles + 3x150	3-5 miles at fast recovery pace + 3x150 @ Nike Campus + NV	NXN run through + Strides. FLW Group 2 miles + Strides	Nike Cross Nationals or Footlocker West Regional

217

High Intensity Interval Training (Hiit) Routine - Core

1. Designed for end of practice.
2. Usually we do a march in place for downs, but as athletes get fit you can cut out downs all together and just do a break in between sets, either way works. Usually 30 second breaks between sets.
3. Remember that these schedules are designed for varsity athletes and should be modified for younger and beginning athletes.

Core HIIT – Routine 1

1. Speed Push-ups
2. Supermans
3. Burpees
4. Speed Crunches
5. Line Jumps

Core HIIT – Routine 2

1. Star Jumps
2. Jackknife
3. Mountain Climbers
4. Jump, Squat, Touch Down
5. Speed Bicycle Crunches

Core HIIT – Routine 3

1. Squats

2. Leg Lifts
3. Jumping Lunges
4. Bear Crawls – 3 forward, 3 back
5. Speed Jumping Jacks

XC Season Core HIIT Build Up

1. Week 1 – 20 seconds up, 10 seconds down – 2 Sets
2. Week 2 - 20 seconds up, 10 seconds down – 2 Sets
3. Week 3 - 20 seconds up, 10 seconds down – 2 Sets
4. Week 4 - 30 seconds up, 15 seconds down – 2 Sets
5. Week 5 - 30 seconds up, 15 seconds down – 2 Sets
6. Week 6 - 30 seconds up, 15 seconds down – 3 Sets
7. Week 7 - 30 seconds up, 15 seconds down – 3 Sets
8. Week 8 - 40 seconds up, 20 seconds down – 2 Sets
9. Week 9 - 40 seconds up, 20 seconds down – 2 Sets
10. Week 10 - 40 seconds up, 20 seconds down – 2 Sets
11. Week 11 - 40 seconds up, 15 seconds down – 2 Sets
12. Week 12 - 40 seconds up, 15 seconds down – 2 Sets
13. Week 13 - 45 seconds up, 20 seconds down – 2 Sets
14. Week 14 - 45 seconds up, 20 seconds down – 2 Sets
15. Week 15 – 45 seconds up, 15 seconds down – 3 Sets
16. Week 16 - 50 seconds up, 20 seconds down – 3 Sets
17. Week 17 - 50 seconds up, 20 seconds down – 3 Sets
18. Week 18 - 50 seconds up, 15 seconds down – 3 Sets
19. Week 19 - 60 seconds up, 30 seconds down – 3 Sets
20. Week 20 - 60 seconds up, 30 seconds down – 3 Sets
21. Week 21 - 60 seconds up, 20 seconds down – 3 Sets

High Intensity Interval Training (Hiit) Routine - Running

1. Warm-up

2. HIIT - A period of high-intensity running (Sprint 96+% of max), and a period of low-intensity running (jog 40-50% of max).

HIITs should always focus on running the ups hard and the offs easy. Make sure to increase duration and intensity throughout the season using the chart above. This is a sprint, not a Vo2 type pace workout. Athletes should be near full speed on the ups.

XC Season Build Up

- Week 1 - 10 seconds Up, 20 seconds Off - 1:00 duration
- Week 2 - 15 seconds Up, 15 seconds Off - 1:30 duration
- Week 3 - 15 seconds Up, 15 seconds Off - 1:30 duration
- Week 4 - 20 seconds Up, 10 seconds Off - 1:30 duration
- Week 5 - 20 seconds Up, 10 seconds Off - 1:30 duration
- Week 6 - 15 seconds Up, 15 seconds Off – 2:00 duration
- Week 7 - 15 seconds Up, 15 seconds Off - 2:00 duration
- Week 8 - 20 seconds Up, 10 seconds Off - 2:00 duration
- Week 9 - 20 seconds Up, 10 seconds Off - 2:00 duration
- Week 10 - 15 seconds Up, 15 seconds Off - 2:30 duration
- Week 11 - 15 seconds Up, 15 seconds Off - 2:30 duration
- Week 12 - 20 seconds Up, 10 seconds Off - 2:30 duration
- Week 13 - 20 seconds Up, 10 seconds Off - 2:30 duration
- Week 14 - 15 seconds Up, 15 seconds Off – 3:00 duration
- Week 15 - 15 seconds Up, 15 seconds Off – 3:00 duration
- Week 16 - 20 seconds Up, 10 seconds Off - 3:00

duration

- Week 17 - 20 seconds Up, 10 seconds Off - 3:00 duration
- Week 18 - 15 seconds Up, 15 seconds Off - 3:30 duration
- Week 19 - 15 seconds Up, 15 seconds Off - 3:30 duration
- Week 20 - 20 seconds Up, 10 seconds Off - 3:30 duration
- Week 21 - 20 seconds Up, 10 seconds Off - 3:30 duration

ACKNOWLEDGEMENT

There are so many people that go into a coaching career that I couldn't possibly name them all here. I would like to take this opportunity to thank a few people that have made this journey an unforgettable one.

To the athletes, without which none of this would be possible. For allowing me to be a guide in your life when you could have chosen to do anything else. For giving your all so that we all could enjoy the sweet taste of victory. For all the miles, all the smiles, and for all the good times we had together, thank you!

To my wife Teresa Soles has been as amazing a coach's wife as is humanly possible. Allowing me long nights, fixations, bad days, and temper tantrums along the way, she has always been my rock. Always there to console me after a loss, and to remind me I'm not that big of a deal after a win. I have been blessed to come home time and time again to someone who truly understands my passion and believes in me no matter what. Thank you and I love you more than words can say!

To my three amazing children; Jordan, London, and Jackson. Your patience with your father being gone so often speaks volumes to the people you will grow up to be. Know that although I was gone a lot working, I was always working hard to give you an amazing life. I hope you believe that I have accomplished that. Know that many of the times I was gone, I was often thinking of you.

My right-hand man Daniel Noble. Every once in a while, our kind Heavenly Father sends us a guardian angel to look over us. Coach Noble gives everything he can to me, and to the athletes in our program. No one will ever truly know the amount of work he puts in, on top of the many other responsibilities he has, but I want him to know that I am forever grateful for his kindness, advice, support, and ability to believe when others did not. You my friend, are as worthy of the Hall of Fame as anyone I have ever met. Thank you for setting the example every single day.

To my mom, Jo Anne Sage, who always taught me to be an independent thinker. She raised me to understand that nothing is given to you, you have to put in the work and you have to want it more than everyone else.

A big thank you to Dr. Steven Webb for his support and belief in me over the years. It has meant the world to me!

Thank you to Martin Dugard, who without his coaxing and assistance I might not have ever decided to sit down and write. To have the help of a bestselling author definitely makes this process a lot less scary. Thank you for your time and patience with me while I embarked on this new adventure in writing.

Thank you to everyone who has be a part of the program over the years and helped to make us the elite program that we are. Athletes, parents, assistant coaches, athletic directors, and friends, I thank you for being an amazing part of our journey!

ABOUT THE AUTHOR

Doug Soles

Coach Doug Soles is one of the top high  school cross country coaches in the country, having won 14 Division 1 State Championships in California. His teams have been on the podium at Nike Cross Nationals 7 times, including winning the national title for the boys in 2015. His teams became the perennial favorites in California cross country, and were consistently ranked in the top 10 in the nation. Coach Soles has been named the National Coach of the Year by the USTFCCCA and USA Today, as well as being named the Girls Cross Country Coach of the Decade for 2010-19 by MaxPreps. He has been a contributor to running websites like Highschoolrunningcoach.com and PodiumRunner.com, and many other media outlets. Coach Soles now lives in Utah with his family and coaches at Herriman High School. In 2022, he took his new team to NXN and finished on the Boys Podium!

Made in the USA
Monee, IL
10 November 2024

69757679R00128